D0906233

BLOOD ON GERMAN SNOW

Joseph G. Dawson III, General Editor

Blood on
German Snow

*An African American Artilleryman
in World War II and Beyond*

Emiel W. Owens

Texas A&M University Press   *College Station*

Library of Congress Cataloging-in-Publication Data

Owens, Emiel W., 1922–

  Blood on German snow : an African American artilleryman in
World War II and beyond / Emiel W. Owens. — 1st ed.
    p. cm. — (Texas A&M University military history series ; #105)
  Includes bibliographical references and index.
  ISBN-13: 978-1-58544-537-0 (cloth : alk. paper)
  ISBN-10: 1-58544-537-1 (cloth : alk. paper)
  1. Owens, Emiel W., 1922– . 2. United States. Army. Field
Artillery Battalion, 777th. 3. World War, 1939–1945—Artillery operations,
American. 4. World War, 1939–1945—Participation, African-American.
5. World War, 1939–1945—Campaigns—Western Front. 6. World War,
1939–1945—Personal narratives, Amercian. 7. Soldiers—United States—
Biography. 8. African American soldiers—Biography. I. Title.
II. Series: Texas A & M University military history series ; 105.
D769.34777th .O94   2006
940.54'8173—dc22   2005037460

Contents

Illustrations

BLOOD ON GERMAN SNOW

Preface

This book details my life as a field artilleryman in the U.S. Army. It is a personal story about what happened to me as a soldier—my training, places I traveled, how I lived, combat experiences in Western Europe, battles I fought, two ocean crossings, and four crossings of the English Channel. It is also about the people I met and a first-person account of war as I witnessed it during three and a half years in the service. The title, *Blood on German Snow,* relates to a battle on Germany's western front in which I took part while my battalion was attached to the XVI Corps and the 35th Infantry Division. The XVI Corps had amassed some five thousand guns on the west bank of the Rhine River in preparation for our crossing. My gun, number 3, Battery B, 777th Field Artillery Battalion, received the task of leading the charge by firing the first rounds at targets on the east side of the river in the town of Mehrum, Germany. In unison the five thousand guns followed, firing for three hours beginning at 1:00 A.M. on March 25, 1945. We ceased firing at 3:00 A.M., commenced crossing the river at 4:00 A.M., and had a bridgehead established on the east side in the vicinity of Verden, Germany, by sunrise.

My story begins with some details of my early life at home, work, and school and finally my induction into the army. I include this information because I believe that background is in many ways crucial in assessing a soldier's capability—particularly with regard to carrying out duties under extremely adverse conditions, where I believe that an individual's values and sense of duty and loyalty are ingrained at an early age. In my case, my home life defined virtue in the classic sense of fortitude and courage.

Part of my story is also about the last conversations I had with my cousin Zelmo Owens, who lived with my two brothers and me at my grandmother's house. His home was in a rural area, so he lived with us to attend high school. In the early part of 1941 the radio airwaves were full of talk of war, and it was on the minds of the people on the streets in my part of Smithville, Texas, in "Low Woods." Zelmo and I would soon be about the right age to fight in a war, and we felt a patriotic duty to serve our country if we were called. We talked and concluded that we had an undying love for our country and would fight and die if need be to defend it, even though we both hated the politics of our racist country. We felt the demeaning attitudes and laws would have to change. After high school, we shook hands, embraced, and parted; Zelmo went directly into the army, while I spent a year in college. We promised to meet again after the war and continue our discussion about the direction our lives would take. I never saw Zelmo again. The brutality of war robbed him of his mind, and he has been in a Veterans Administration mental health facility for more than sixty years.

My story ends with some details of my life activities after being discharged from the army, which includes marriage and family formation, academic achievements, and work experiences. I am now in the waning years of my life but still optimistic about the future. I have had time with goodness on my side to endow me with a loftiness of purpose and a sense of moral heroism worth a lifetime of contentment and security. Is it not true that the evening of a well-spent life brings its own lamps? I think so.

I wish to express my profound gratitude to those who assisted me in bringing together research necessary for the completion of this book. These individuals and organizations include M. A. Gedra, Modern Military Records (NWCTM), National Archives, Trust Fund, Washington D.C.; Marilyn Holt, Carnegie Library of Pittsburgh, Pittsburgh, Pennsylvania; Sgt. Dena Everett, executive assistant, U.S. Army Center of Military History, Fort McNair, Washington, D.C.; Charlene Neuwiller, archivist, and Lisa Jacofus, archivist assistant, *European Stars and Stripes*, Washington, D.C.; and Fort Sill Oklahoma Museum, Lawton, Oklahoma. Very special thanks go to my assistant, Jennifer Harrison, who prepared the original manuscript, and to Fannie Burt for her most valuable editorial assistance. I am truly grateful to Roger Cirello of the Association of the United States Army (AUSA) for his willingness to accept my manuscript as a subject in his manuscript portfolio and to search for publication outlets. Finally, I want to express my sincere thanks to Mary Lenn Dixon, editor-in-chief, Thom Lemmons, managing editor, and other members of Texas A&M University Press, including Leanna M. Pate, exhibitions and special promotions manager; Linda Salitros, assistant to the director; and Diana Vance, acquisitions assistant, for helping me bring this manuscript to the production stage and for their promotion efforts. Then I want to thank Hattie, my wife, for her patience.

CHAPTER 1

A Typical African American and a U.S. Citizen

My early life was typical for a Southern, rural African American born in the United States in 1922. My father, mother, two brothers, one sister, and I lived on a farm as sharecroppers for a large landowner. Our house was situated near the Colorado River, so close in fact that on occasion I could hear the roar of the flowing water, and at times the water would rise and creep dangerously near our house. During one such episode I asked my father, "What are rivers and where do they come from?" Despite having had only a fourth-grade education, he summed up the intricacies of rivers using his own language, combined with a surprisingly vast knowledge of rivers both in the United States and throughout the world. He had such detailed information that he must have had an excellent geography teacher.

I remember hearing my parents having conversations about field work from a time when I must have been about five years old, but I do not recall going to a field at this very early age, even though I must have spent much of my time there. However, some memories are extremely vivid. I remember my brother and sister hiding in a closet one day in fear of a wild animal entering our house.

We had a barn and a feedlot where Daddy kept his work mules and our farm equipment, which consisted of a plow and a seed planter. My mother had a round, black iron pot under which she would build a fire to wash our clothes. She kept a small iron bar nearby that she used as a poker to stir our clothes while they boiled. In the evenings, primarily on weekends, other sharecroppers would come to our house, and along with my dad, would engage in target practice with 22-caliber rifles. With what I am sure today would be rated as marksman aim, they practiced and entertained themselves by shooting match stems off posts. They also put their skills to practical use by hunting rabbits, squirrels, and other wild animals as sources of meat. Life was simple here—hard field work offset by small gatherings as a source of some pleasure.

There is, however, one event I can remember that in hindsight could have caused a devastating blow to my family. Apparently, as many young children do, I had a bad habit of always putting things in my mouth, such as pennies and anything tiny and handy that I could get my hands on. My mother was constantly scolding me for this habit. One night, despite the warnings, I sat on our back porch with an open safety pin in my mouth taking in the adult goings-on. Suddenly, a decayed board broke and I fell through to the ground. With the impact of hitting the ground, I swallowed the open safety pin, lodging it in my throat with the open portion facing the front of my mouth. When my mother heard my gagging, she screamed and started calling to my dad, who was in the feedlot with our work mules. He rushed to me, jammed his fingers into my already open mouth, and pulled the pin out, flesh and all. In spite of my mouth being full of blood, my dad filled it with lard from a slaughtered pig. The bleeding soon stopped, and my throat and mouth healed with no apparent permanent damage. No more things went to my mouth after this mishap, and a possible disaster was diverted; but this seemingly tranquil life was soon to be plagued with upheaval of a more frightening kind.

Two of the sharecroppers were white and lived on farms adjoining those of black sharecroppers. This caused them to share some of the weekend shooting pleasures of the black sharecroppers. I heard my dad tell my mother about a rumor floating around the farms that there was some kind of sexual activity going on between one of the white sharecroppers and the wife of a black sharecropper named Mit Welburn. When word spread that the sexual sharing was mutual and that Mit was having an affair with the same white sharecropper's wife (a sort of spouse-swapping arrangement), white sharecroppers and farmers from the surrounding communities became hostile and organized a group to catch and lynch Mit. The mob surrounded Mit's house and got close enough to him to knock his front teeth out, but Mit escaped with the help of the white sharecropper.

However, as content as we may have been with our lifestyle there, as things often end up for sharecroppers, soon after this event and at the end of the crop season, Daddy left the farm and moved to town. There he worked as a spike man laying railroad ties. The white sharecropper also left the farm, moved to town, and began to work for the railroad. There his wife gave birth to a girl with a light complexion—a typical "mulatto" girl, as was the commonly used term in those days.

Life for me changed after leaving the farm and moving to Washington Street in Smithville. I found most of the boys my age in the streets in groups during the evenings shooting marbles. I never had that much free time, as after I completed my homework, my mother would sit on the floor and teach me to count money.

My mother set the tone of all our family activities. There were a few discussions and activities that we engaged in with her that stand out in my memory today. I remember her telling us that she wanted us to be too highly educated to live in Texas. She thought that Jim Crow Texas would not provide the facilities for her children to develop to their fullest potential. Nor would they have the employment opportunities to afford the living standard she had in mind for her children. I thought she stayed happy as a housewife, since she would walk through our house singing all the time. Her favorite song was "In the Garden," which I catch myself singing during unguarded moments even today. The song begins, "I come to the garden alone, while the dew is still on the roses." I kept thinking her singing continuously was an expression of happiness, but now I am not sure.

On Saturday, Daddy would cut the logs the hired labor had brought in during the week and sell the wood to families for cooking on wood stoves and for heating their homes during the winter. Daddy rigged up a saw attached to a Model T Ford engine with a puller and belt. He then would put a log about six feet long on a small platform, gradually raise it up to the turning saw, and cut the log into a piece about a foot long. This length made each block ideal for inserting into wood stoves. Wood then was sold to customers by the cord—blocks of wood stacked four feet wide, four feet high, and eight feet long. At the time, a cord of wood sold for about five dollars. My job was to feed the engine by observing the size of log to be cut and open the carburetor on the Ford engine accordingly. That required real concentration for an eleven-year-old. On Saturday, when I was not "feeding the engine," we would go to the woods with handsaws and axes to cut down trees, trim them up, and haul them in as logs for cutting into cordwood. In spite of the hard work, life was good for us and we felt happy and protected.

Then tension began to grow in our family. I was not sure about the causes, but I could see the attitude between my mother and father changing, which was troubling. The world seemingly was falling apart, even coming to an end. In spite of the differences they were having, my parents continued to keep track and observe our tendencies for future development. Charles, my oldest brother, was thirteen and showing mechanical tendencies; I liked plants and the science of biology; and my sister, Volma, was leaning toward music; but it was too early to tell in what direction my youngest brother, Clarence, was leaning.

A recent *Time* magazine article claimed that each individual reaches one pinnacle of happiness during a lifetime. As I look back over my childhood, in spite of the adversities, I cannot find any experience that I would change if I were granted the opportunity. The events of those early years made me the adult I am today.

About My Hometown

My hometown, Smithville, is in Central Texas on the banks of the Colorado River, approximately forty miles east of the city of Austin. The citizens of Smithville, which is located among the "Lost Pines of Texas," not only enjoy the beautiful pines but relish the shade of many old oak and pecan trees.

The village of Old Smithville was laid out on 640 acres of land granted to two settlers, Thomas J. Gozely and Lewis Lomas. The settlement was called Smithville in honor of pioneer settler William Smith. The Taylor, Bastrop, and Houston Railroad, later a part of the Missouri, Kansas, and Texas System (MKT/Katy), arrived in 1886, and the town grew up between the tracks and the river. Smithville began as a railroad town. The railroad tracks that ran through it became the town's racial divide, splitting it into two parts.

North of the "round house," where train engines were repaired and the railroad station was located, the whites lived. Colored Town was on the south side, running from the round house all the way to Zapalac's field on the south end. One prominent street in Colored Town was Washington Street, which was wider than all the others and had a gravel surface. Its occupants were predominantly light-skinned blacks who lived in the larger white houses with landscaped beds of perennials called "four o'clocks." Despite my family's dark complexion, we lived on Washington Street, as Daddy was a railroad laborer. Persimmon and plum granite trees, as well as four o'clock plants, dominated the landscape around our house. This area of town consisted of railroad workers, owners of small businesses, and porters and semiskilled workers: the colored middle class.

Our house was L shaped with a long porch extending the length of the rear rooms. The house was built on the center of three lots, and my dad stored cordwood on the lot to the left of our home. On the lot to the right, Daddy planted sweet potato slips from which the vines grew. I had sweet potatoes every day in some form for as long as I can remember during my early life. A meal is incomplete for me, even today, without a serving of sweet potatoes. I even describe the beauty of a sunrise as a flash of splendor with

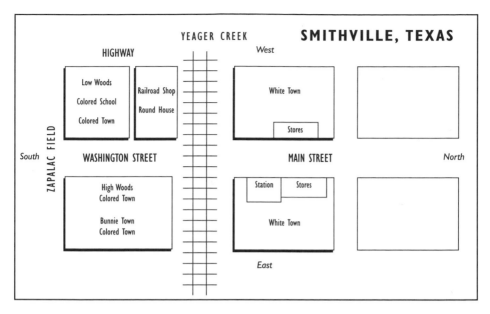

Diagram of Smithville, Texas, during the 1920s–1940s.

blazing scarlet clouds on the shaft of light in terms of sweet potato clouds. My dad brought some of his sharecropping activities and habits with him to town and to Washington Street.

At the same time, he worked as a railroad laborer who laid the cross ties and tracks. When I was a child, I often stood and watched the railroad workers hit spikes in a rhythmic pattern as those who tapped, and those waiting in the wings to tap, kept the rhythm: "Hit it is / hit it is / Yo man I'm gone again." To watch two dozen men hit spikes in unison and keep a rhythm fascinated me. I can still hear the ring of the tapping in my ears.

A piece of steel from one of the spikes hit Daddy in the left arm and embedded just above the elbow, so he was transferred to the round house. One of his jobs in the round house was to fill an elevated sandbox located near the tracks, where locomotives could pull under and receive sand in a designated container on the locomotive. When steam engines were pulling a large number of boxcars and trying to go up an incline, the wheels would slip as they tried to gain traction. When loaded on the locomotive, the sand was funneled down through a tube in front of the wheels when the locomotive needed traction. My brother Charles and I would help our father by shoveling sand and filling the box for him after school. I enjoyed sitting at the railroad crossing with inclines, watching locomotives spinning wheels struggling for traction and securing it when the sand was let down on the track. There is still a fascination today. These were middle-income activities that set Washington Street coloreds apart from the other coloreds in town.

From Washington Street, the area five blocks east and west to the colored school on the west side was called "High Woods." The area west of the school to the end of town at Yeager Creek was called "Low Woods." Here, domestic servants, farm laborers, maids, and laborers for other businesses lived. My paternal grandmother lived in Low Woods. About five blocks east of High Woods was the area called "Bunnie Town." This was also where common laborers lived. They were mostly hunters of game such as rabbits and squirrels. Each family usually had hunting dogs, such as greyhounds. Their occupation distinguished them from the people of High Woods.

My hometown is a place where churches are important, neighbors are cohesive, and newspapers, a bit folksy, seem to print only positive news. Smithville is still what all of America used to be—a place where the problems of society are simpler and sometimes resolved over morning coffee.

There were five main churches in Smithville. Those who lived on Washington Street in High Woods attended the First Baptist and Methodist; Low Woods households attended the Second Baptist. Those who attended Holy Church were a special group and hard to classify by geographic location; all members went their separate ways after church. Before my parents divorced, my family attended the Second Baptist Church, meaning that we lived in High Woods but had more of the traits common to people of Low Woods.

My parents divorced when I was twelve, and my two brothers and I moved to Low Woods to live with my grandmother. Life went on for us after the divorce. Our grandmother gave us all the love and tender care we could hope for, but still life seemed to be going downhill. Just as she had taken me and my two brothers in after our parents' divorce, she also took in my uncle's two children as well as two of my other cousins. We all lived with her and went to school. Grandmother's house was a one-bedroom structure with a small living room, a breakfast room, and small kitchen with a wood stove for food preparation. Somehow, we all managed to live there. One positive result of my having survived this living experience is that I am very organized around home today. We did not have closets but used nails for hanging our school, everyday, and Sunday clothes. So many people could not have functioned in such limited space without organization.

The primary memory I have of living with my grandmother is that her front door was never locked. The Low Woods society had more of a communal system of sharing—whatever resources you had were equally available to a neighbor in need. That meant that poverty was a relative position in society, and no one felt its full impact.

The piece of steel in my dad's arm gave him trouble later on, and he sued the railroad. The railroad paid him for the injury but blackballed him for suing, and he never worked for them again. Just before he left railroad employment, I would take his lunch to him as he was working on the evening shift. I would usually get to the round house where he worked about 5:00 P.M.. Each evening upon my arrival, I would meet a mulatto girl also bringing lunch to her father, who was white. She was no different from the mulatto families living on my street. She approached the round house from the north side, where the whites lived, instead of from the south or the colored neighborhood. I was told later that she was the daughter of Mit Welburn, the black former sharecropper, and the wife of the white sharecropper. I took lunch to Daddy one evening and did not see her. She had finished elementary school and was not allowed to attend the white high school so had been sent to a Northern state to attend high school. I understand she later married a white man there.

In a Jim Crow environment as prevailed in my hometown, contact between whites and coloreds was usually through either schools and teachers or the servitude route. My first contact of any kind with whites occurred when I delivered laundry to a white family after the clothes had been washed and ironed by my grandmother. In this relation, the white people were friendly. They would send messages occasionally to my grandmother telling her that her "grandsons were very special boys." This friendly attitude prevailed among the whites with whom we came in contact. In later years after my return from the army, I had an encounter showing the racist side of the Smithville society.

My second day home after being discharged from the army, I decided to attend a movie. There was just one movie theater in town, and I had attended it throughout my early years. In the theater, the whites would sit on the first floor and the coloreds in the balcony. There were two doors entering the theater. The one to the right led primarily downstairs where the whites sat. Through this door and to the left led upstairs to the balcony. The door to the left, however, led directly to the balcony. Attending the movie on this occasion was my first time in about four years. As I walked in, I purchased my ticket and a bag of popcorn. The popcorn machine was located near the right-hand door. Unconsciously, I walked through the right-hand door and was turning left to go to the balcony when a man yelled, "Boy, don't go through that door; you go to the balcony." His tone was threatening.

I turned around and confronted the man, who I think was the manager, telling him not to ever yell at me and call me "boy" again. I got closer to him and asked, "Did you hear me?" He did not respond. I got closer to him and asked him again, "Did you hear me?"

He responded, "I did." I then told him to give me my money back for the ticket and popcorn. I got my money and walked out. One teenager in the small lobby recognized me and called my mother to tell her about the incident. My mother was upset, but less so after I explained exactly what had happened. I left Smithville two days later, returning to school at Prairie View, where I had enrolled for the spring semester.

When I drove back to my hometown recently, I was curious to see how it had changed physically after my being away for so many years. But I was more interested in whether its spirit had altered. Most of the Smithvillians I talked to said the forty-mile distance from Austin buffers the town. There have been changes, of course, but the town's essence remains the same. The exception is the integration of schools and public places. Mit Welburn's little daughter would no longer be forced to leave home and go up North to finish high school simply because her mother was white and her father was black.

I went to the movie that night, walked in, bought some popcorn, walked through the right-hand entrance door, and immediately turned left to go upstairs to the balcony. This was my spontaneous reaction in spite of having the opportunity to sit wherever I wanted. The old force of habit surfaced.

It was a warm day, so after the movie I stopped at the drugstore on Main Street to get a soft drink. While I was sitting at the table, it kept coming to my mind that this place was exclusively for whites when I was growing up. After being there for about five minutes, I was joined by a white couple, seemingly in their early sixties. They too had spent their early life here but moved away and were home on a visit. The gentleman, Thomas, related to me, "During my early marriage, I came home with my new bride. Our memories of Smithville are only partially built of masonry. When we remember Smithville, we first think of its ability to attract, nurture, and tolerate eccentricity. A bird lady lived just outside Smithville city limits. She would cover herself with leaves and watch birds for hours. On Thanksgiving she fashioned a pilgrim out of mashed seed, baked it, and invited turkeys to feast on the carcass. She then just disappeared."

CHAPTER 1

Another couple who lived here and later moved away said, "We have spent the time since we left Smithville trying to understand why it was such a good town. We've narrowed it to these attributes: People danced often; people were intensely, almost insanely social; few weekends passed without a public barbecue." One citizen volunteered that he believed that no place had more people doing more things in voluntary public service than in Smithville.

Many people had never heard of my hometown until after seeing the movie *Hope Floats*, which was made about life in Smithville and filmed there. As one character in the movie says, "Smithville was not on any map until we got to Texas." You get the feeling that, as in the movie, traditional values are still deeply embedded here. So are all the other facets of small-town life. Families are strong, everyone knows everybody, and the majority of the population remembers you from childhood.

Today my hometown is still a quiet place where kids walk safely to school, where neighbors look out for them and report back if they misbehave. Although minus passenger trains, many Smithville residents still work for the railroad. If you should visit sometime in the future, before leaving, you should stop at all the *Hope Floats* movie filming locations—the employment office, Honey's Diner, and the house at the end of Olive Street. Except for the house, all are merely signs on empty buildings now, souvenirs of the day the world discovered my hometown, Smithville.

Truck Hauls Diversity

Having lost his job with the railroad, my dad expanded his trucking activities as a means of making a living. He had a truck fitted with different beds to be used with his various enterprises. One bed was used to haul cedar logs, which we cut and loaded, to the mill. Another truck bed was used to haul scrap iron, which we helped load, to Houston. We rode with him on Friday nights and Saturdays. Still another truck bed was used to pick up people to take on "cotton picks" during the summer cotton-picking season. All the labor needed for picking the local cotton crop was found in Low Woods. My dad made the cab for our truck out of sheet metal. The cab had no doors. How we endured the cold nights on the road and did not fall out of the cab as we slept, I just do not know. It frightens me just to think about it today. The risks and discomforts of long hauls impacted my attitude and gave me courage. I thought my dad would manage to take care of us—we never rented, we always had a place we called home, and we always had hired labor to help run Daddy's various enterprises.

The bed on the iron truck could be replaced with a dump bed for hauling sand and gravel, particularly for the highway department. I was fourteen at the time and helped haul sand and gravel in the evenings and on weekends. One contract meant a one-way haul of thirty-five miles between the gravel pit and the highway being built. A day's work for Daddy and eight other drivers was to haul ten loads of gravel, but one white driver made eleven loads; that is, he would double up on us near the last load for the day.

I was helping my dad drive and did not believe the white driver should be able to beat us to the gravel pit, as his truck was one year older. We both drove Chevrolet trucks: ours was a 1936 model and his was a 1935 model. I set the day in my mind to challenge him, without Daddy knowing my intentions. I tailed the white driver load for load throughout the day, just far enough behind to keep him from suspecting my intentions.

During the day I had studied the topography of the highway and knew the slopes where there would be less traffic to challenge and pass him. Late that evening, with the sun to our back and a clear highway for a mile, I made my move. Daddy was asleep. The white driver saw my truck directly behind him as I drew near, but he did not recognize me because I was so small under the wheel, so he maintained his speed. We were about five miles from the gravel pit, and whoever got there first would receive the last load for the day. During those years, trucks lacked acceleration power. As I pulled to go around him, he recognized the truck and tried to pick up speed. I had the momentum and was gradually passing him. As I got even with him, face-to-face, he looked over at me with disdain and determination, perspiration flowing down his face. The rear of my bed was at the front of his truck when the speed and the noise of the two trucks awakened my dad. He quickly recognized what was taking place and forced me to slow down and let the white man's truck go out in front. The white man went ahead and kept his usual pattern of making one load more than the other drivers.

I had a problem with this and kept wondering why I had to slow down and make less money than we were capable of making. I later thought my dad was afraid of a racial encounter at the gravel pit, as racial injustice was rampant during this era. As I pass the gravel pit and this particular stretch of the highway after all these years, I still wonder why I had to let the white driver beat me. I thought this action was out of character for my dad. The white driver continued to make the extra load each day. From that point on, whenever our truck would meet up at the gravel pit, the white driver would always stare straight at me. He knew that I had him beat that day in spite of being only a fourteen-year-old kid. I think that possibly deflated his ego as the top truck hauler. A week later this gravel-hauling contract was completed. It was time for us to change beds on our truck and get ready for our "cotton pick."

The "Cotton Pick"

The summer months signaled the time for my dad to carry cotton pickers (often referred to as hands) to South Texas. He would pick up his crew of thirty to forty people in Low Woods and follow the South Texas pick during June, July, and August and then move to West Texas for September, October, and November. I did not make the West Texas pick, as school started in late August. As crew chief, my dad contracted growers who had cotton to pick, transported the pickers, and made arrangements with the growers for housing and all the other meager needs of cotton pickers. Housing was very accessible—one-room shanties were located in the middle of the cotton fields. In addition, he hauled the pickers to the field, weighed the cotton each worker picked, loaded the picked cotton on his truck, and hauled it to the gin where it was cleaned and baled. A bale weighs about fifteen hundred pounds. The South Texas cotton differed from cotton in most other fields—it had been irrigated and was very tall. Rather than bend over and pick "down" as is done with cotton grown on short stalks, pickers pick "up" because the cotton stalks are taller than waist high.

For some reason, snakes were numerous in the fields. There were venomous rattlesnakes, which were usually found in dry, hot climates such as that in West Texas. All pickers received a ten-foot-long sack to strap across their shoulders. The sack had dual functions. During the day it held the picked cotton, and at night it became a sleeping mattress.

Cotton blossoms are white. They grow into green bolls that ripen and pop open to reveal glossy white streams of cotton. A cotton field gives the impression of a stream of long, white cloth. The fields are planted in rows about two miles long. In the first rows, the blossoms are bigger beneath the canopy of green cotton leaves, giving the picker a picture of almost a cotton heaven. I took the first two rows. "I'm taking the third and fourth rows," my brother Charles asserted, moving toward them.

All forty hands spread out. We started on eighty rows with sack straps laced across our shoulders as we pulled the long white sacks. It was just about dawn, and as the sun broke over the horizon, it filtered through the leaves of the cotton stalks and made lacy patterns on the ground. I began picking, rotating from row to row without any loss of hand motion. By the end of the row, each of our sacks was full with about sixty pounds of cotton. The truck was parked at the end of the row where my dad weighed each sack and then loaded it on his truck to haul to the gin. "You have fifty-five pounds," he told me after weighing my sack.

One picker, sitting on his sack waiting for it to be weighed, leaned back to pull a stalk of cotton over his head for a little protection against the burning sun. Suddenly, he jumped up and began running and pointing toward his chest, screaming, "I've been bitten!" Panic and fear were in his wide-open, helpless eyes. Then I saw the culprit. A diamondback rattler had bitten him—the snake's fangs were still embedded in his chest. The picker managed to free himself of the rattler but kept running until I caught and overpowered him.

Fearful and gasping for breath, he asked, "Will I die?"

"We will get you to a doctor and keep you alive," I reassured him.

However, we knew that his running had caused the poisonous venom to spread quickly throughout his body. I emptied the cotton out of my sack and used it as a gurney. Two of us put him on my sack so that we could carry him back to our shanty. Inside, we laid him on the floor, where I noticed, for the first time, a brown greasy coating on the floor soil and grease dripped and pounded over the years by earlier pickers. His breathing became irregular with short gasps. His body soon turned blue.

All night, pickers sat motionless and kept watch over the young man. The stillness was broken only occasionally by a few words of a mournful hymn by an older female picker and a lingering rattle in the throat of the dying young man. As she sang almost inaudibly, the young picker opened his eyes briefly at intervals, as if he could hear more of the mournful spiritual than we could, and that perhaps was lifting his spirit. I believe the spiritual was "Precious Lord." I remember the line "Precious Lord, take my hand, lead me on, let me stand." An owl—my grandmother used to call them death owls—shrilled all through the night in the chinaberry tree near our shanty. It had become clear to me now that despite our hopes, death was not far away. Everyone kept close vigilance all night. I constantly and nervously looked for signs of death. The horseshoe over our front door would keep the spirit of those already touched by death from coming into our house, according to a common legend, but the superstition was no guarantee that it would keep death itself from visiting.

We could not save him. He died at sunrise. The dead picker was only sixteen, and the other pickers thought that many more young people in the crew could be lost to the same fate. The young man's body was placed in a body bag and shipped back to Low Woods for burial.

CHAPTER 1

Symbolically, as a last rite, bolls of cotton were placed on coffins of fallen cotton pickers as they were lowered for burial. Sixteen bolls were shipped in the young picker's body bag. "Somehow if you can see the light of daybreak," an unknown picker uttered, "it takes away the fear of dying."

No one picked cotton the day after the tragic death. The grower came by and was troubled at the threat of the pickers leaving the field because of the danger. I looked up and saw railroad boxcars backing into the field on tracks two hundred yards from where we had been picking cotton the day before. I thought that cotton would be loaded from the crew chief's truck to the boxcars and then sent to the gin. This, I believed, would eliminate the crew chief's taking time to drive to the gin, thus keeping the truck in the field for loading after the sacks were weighed. Men began unloading long boxes out of the boxcars and taking the tops off them. Again, I thought the sacks of cotton we picked would be emptied into the boxes for convenience. To my amazement, they were releasing long snakes with red and black bands into the field. The cotton pickers were frightened, but these snakes were nonpoisonous king snakes released into the field as predators to kill rattlesnakes.

I came to the field one morning at sunrise to get an early start at a time when the sun was still friendly. I was in the rhythm of picking cotton on two rows, and, to my horror, about halfway down the row I stepped on a long red-and-black snake lying in the middle below the canopy of white cotton and green leaves. The snake was also surprised and indecisive about how to react. It curled partially, took a combative stance by raising its head to a striking position, and then just crawled off. I sat on my sack for a few minutes in disbelief. I finished my rows and came to the conclusion that this would be my last season on the cotton pick. There had to be better work available with less risk!

I finished the cotton pick in late August as the crew prepared to shift to West Texas. It was time for me to return for my senior year in high school. The cotton pick was never the same after the death of the young picker, although I learned a lot and had saved a little money for school. Times were hard. My last school year was important to me because I was making preparations for college and had a chance of being the valedictorian of my class.

Senior Year in High School

Smithville Colored High School was part of the Smithville Independent School District. Our school spirit was always extremely high. I was proud of my high school and was a model student. In spite of feeling proud, deep down inside I always felt that I was being shortchanged by the curriculum being offered Negro students. I had a feeling that our academic program should have been more inclusive.

My mother always said that she was a high school graduate. I later discovered that she had only completed the eighth grade, which entitled her to a high school diploma during her time. During my generation, the requirement for a high school diploma had been raised to grade 11 for colored students and consisted of eight full months of school each year. For white students, the requirement for a high school diploma was completion of grade 12 and nine full months of school each year. This meant that at the time of graduation, white students had fulfilled approximately two more years of school than colored students had, which was a tremendous educational advantage. There was no logical reason for such disparity in school other than giving white students advantages in a racist system. I think they were afraid of the competition if equal academic opportunities were offered to all children in the state of Texas.

Our textbooks were supplied by the Smithville Independent School District. We were issued books at the beginning of each year, which were returned at the end of the term. During my eleven years of school I do not ever remember being issued a brand-new textbook. Our books were always used, and by the time we received them, they were partially out of date. They were worn and tattered and also had "foreign names," such as former book users John Scherosky and Paul Zapalac.

In spite of these disparities I still always felt that I could perform as well as or better than many white students my age. I did not know it then, but later I would have the opportunity to confirm this belief as my superior academic performance was officially recognized.

My senior year was a time of bonding for me. I realized that the class was about to break up and the students I had known since the first grade would be leaving. I remember one morning that the school principal called my name over the loudspeaker, summoning me to his office. I was a bit apprehensive because being called to the principal's office usually meant some sort of punishment would be handed out.

On a prior morning during a class change, I was walking through the auditorium, and as I looked up, I was nearing the principal's daughter along with some other students about to pass me going in the opposite direction. I threw my left arm out to get the attention of a student in the group. My third-grade teacher saw this from across the auditorium and reported I had

CHAPTER 1

my arm around Louise, the principal's daughter. I was called into the office and given three lashes in spite of my attempt to explain what really happened.

Another day I was in class and again received the dreaded summons to the principal's office. My heart pounded as I walked in, and the principal pushed a cane-bottom chair in my direction and asked me to take a seat. After the three lashes from my previous summons to his office, I could not imagine what he wanted to talk with me about. There had not been any school violations—I was extremely careful about that. He began the conversation by telling me that I had been a good student and had led my class in scoring high grades since the first grade. I had been selected as the valedictorian of my class. I instantly felt strangely vindicated, knowing what a struggle my last eleven years had been, especially the devastating impact of my parents' divorce, not to mention having to move to Low Woods.

On the night of graduation I gave my valedictorian address. I told my class and the audience that standing before them was both the happiest and saddest moment of my life and that I was pleased to be graduating but sad about the idea of leaving my classmates of the past eleven years. I also recall saying that "we would in time come back to Smithville Colored High, but we would find students making other and different footprints in the sands of time." My address was short and concluded with Kipling's poem "If," which ends with this stanza:

If you can fill the unforgiving minute
With sixty seconds' worth of distance run,
Yours is the Earth and everything that's in it,
And—which is more—you'll be a Man, my son!

I received a standing ovation. Strangely, for the first time as I sat down, I began thinking about the future and what it held for me. Passages from "If" inspired me, but I had no idea that in the near future I would have to draw on them for the hope and courage I needed to overcome some of the dire situations in which I would find myself. There were rumors floating around about a war that could start any day in Europe. The United States could be drawn into it, but in my world that was so far away, a European war carried no real meaning to me. I would occasionally go to movies, and the newsreels showed a man called Hitler talking to crowds of people. He was always perspiring profusely from the energy he was putting into his discussion. I could not understand German, but his body language reminded me

Graduation, May 24, 1940.
Smithville Colored High School.
Photograph taken the day after
graduation.

of our Baptist minister when he was at the high point of his sermon. As a result, I had mixed feelings about Hitler in spite of the negative comments being presented by the newsreel.

After graduation, my summer routine was the same as usual, hauling scrap iron to Houston, digging to find iron buried under trash during the week, and cutting cedar logs and hauling them to the mill. I knew, however, that this monotony would soon give way to the excitement of my next life adventure—leaving home for the first time to attend college.

Off to College

On September 8, 1940, my cousin Clinton drove me to Prairie View A&M College to enroll for the fall semester. My dad was with his pickers in West Texas and would not return home until late October. Prairie View was a small college of about four thousand students but seemed large to me. I enrolled for sixteen credit hours plus three hours of ROTC. I also worked part-time in the dining hall as a waiter. Considering the adjustment I had to make, the year went along smoothly. Prairie View was almost like a mother hen for many of its impoverished students, such as myself, in that we were not only taught academics but also the social graces and many of the other social arts of living. I learned a lot.

During the spring semester of 1941, I increased my credit load to eighteen hours and made the honor roll. I wanted to increase my credit load so I could enhance my chance of graduation on time in case we were drawn into a war. During the fall semester of 1941, I continued my credit load of eighteen hours and had reasonable success as defensive back on our football team, although I did not have the playing time necessary to letter during my freshman year. I had met a girl on campus during the spring of 1941. Her name was Lillian Brown, and she was an English major from Houston. This was my first try at a courtship since being in college. I had begun to enjoy college life.

With horticulture as my major, I also joined the New Farmers of America Organization. Most of my freshmen classmates spent a great deal of time in the ROTC program, but somehow I could never develop a real interest in the army. To me, the army was a school where obedience was taught, discipline was enforced, and "courage" in the traditional sense of the word

Prairie View New Farmers of America (NFA). The NFA was the segregated part of the Future Farmers of America (FFA). It is an organization primarily for students majoring in agricultural education who will one day become teachers. Students with majors in plant science tend to maintain a membership in the organization. Standing in the third row on the right side is O. T. Thomas, professor of agricultural education and one of the supervisors.

was the name of the game. Besides, I thought at the time, I was still engaged in what I believed to be the most important battle of all—working to make my future better after having struggled for so long in the past—so this thesis did not exactly fit my mode. Unless, of course, there was an emergency, in which case I would be willing to put it all to the test.

I remember walking out of my dormitory on the morning of December 7, 1941, and hearing a radio playing loudly from a room on the ground floor. All of a sudden the music stopped, and a special announcement was made that the Japanese navy had struck Pearl Harbor, which could mean a war between Japan and the United States. There was excitement in the voice of the announcer, but it meant little to me, as I knew nothing of where Pearl Harbor was and what it meant to this country—in spite of my being a freshman in college. By the time I reached the dining hall, students were crowded around radios, listening to the significance of this attack as explained by some ROTC officers. Later in the evening the ROTC was called together in formation by Col. West A. Hamilton, the corps commander.

By this time, President Roosevelt was giving a radio talk to the nation and was declaring war on Japan. Colonel Hamilton explained to our corps that in all likelihood, we would soon be called for military duty and our ROTC training would give us a head start. He thought we would be allowed to complete the fall 1942 and spring 1943 semesters before being called up for duty. We also were told of our option of volunteering and the possibility that many of us could remain together as a unit.

During the spring semester of 1942, there were visible signs of the demand of the armed forces on our senior-level male student population. On campus a garden was reserved as a place for seniors to meet and socialize, and by the fall of 1942 the garden was void of male students. Classes went on as usual, but the center of discussion was the draft and the progress our armed forces were making in the field of battle. Many of our ROTC officers had been drafted and were with combat units in North Africa. I remember going to chapel one Sunday morning, and Rev. Lee C. Phillips, our college chaplain, took as his topic "Life Is But a Bundle of Unfinished Business." He linked it to the war and each individual's responsibility to support it. By the spring semester of 1943, I increased my course load to twenty hours, as I was sure this would be my last semester before going into the army. By this time it was difficult to maintain a class, as so many of the juniors and seniors continually were being drafted into the army. By the spring semester of 1943, my cumulative number of credit hours was 106. For graduation, 140 credit hours were required.

On May 10, 1943, we were called out on our training field and given the orders to report to Fort Sam Houston Reception Center, San Antonio, Texas, for induction into the army. We had two days to get to Fort Sam Houston, so I went home for a day to spend some time with my grandmother, mother, and dad before leaving. This was a sad occasion, even though they had become accustomed to my being away at Prairie View; the uncertainties of the army left them with mixed feelings. My older brother, Charles, had already been inducted and had been shipped to North Africa.

CHAPTER 2

So You're in the Army Now: Training

On May 12, 1943, I said good-bye and caught the train from home, arriving at Fort Sam Houston four hours later. On my first day I was assigned to a barrack, given a physical examination, interviewed, and fitted for an army khaki uniform. As part of my interview, the sergeant wanted to know what I had been doing other than school and, in particular, if I hunted or had experience shooting a rifle. I recounted to him that my dad had given my two brothers and me 410-gauge shotguns at the age of fourteen and that we had hunted rabbits, squirrels, and ducks on ponds—not as a sport but for economic survival. At the end of the interview I received a handbook on army regulations and was told I would possibly become a field artilleryman.

The barrack I was assigned to was a two-story building. Inside, rows of iron bunk beds lined both sides of a big open room, leaving an aisle in the middle. I took my duffel bag of clothes and headed to my assigned bed, labeled "K." I remember laying my duffel bag on my bed and opening it. I had two green uniforms for daily use while training and two brown khaki uniforms for use on weekends if on pass to town. An army steel helmet was to be worn with my green uniform, and a khaki cap with my khaki uniform. But I learned that the khaki cap held a special significance, for the red trim encircling the brim represented my status as field artillery. Each branch of service has its individual trim color, and right away I began to feel an actual sense of pride about the service upon which I was about to embark.

The barrack was filling up by this time, and looking down the aisle, I was pleased to see that my classmate and friend Frederick Moseley had been assigned to the same branch of service and was just four beds away. As I sat on my bed unpacking my bag and glancing briefly at the army regulations book, I noticed that not only was there a 10:00 P.M. curfew but that lights out was also at 10:00 P.M.. True to the manual, that night, and every one thereafter, just a few minutes before 10:00 the lights blinked, and five minutes later they went out. A bugle player would stand in the center of a series of barracks and play "Taps," and all the new recruits who had been talking

Induction into the army at Fort Sam Houston, Texas, May 11, 1943.

and laughing stopped; there was dead silence. The initial silence might give the impression upon entering the barracks that these young soldiers were all sleeping peacefully as if in the dead of the night. Shafts of light were shining through the windows on the west side, but all was silent. To my mind came the scene of being in my grandmother's home and hearing the shrill sound of what she called death owls, which, according to her, predicted the passing of a soul. A few hours later, usually late in the night after we heard these sounds, the church bell would give a mournful toll, indicating that a soul had indeed "passed on into the clouds" as my grandmother had foretold. The last time I had even thought of the death owls was when that sixteen-year-old picker died and I heard the shrieks—now that seemed so long ago.

When "Taps" finished, the only light in the barrack was the night-light shining through the windows. After the initial silence, it became clear that there was not a dry eye in the entire place. A few of the recruits were crying aloud but most in silence. I am not sure why they were crying. Was it fear, or did the shrill sound of "Taps" make them lonely? This was the first night most of them had been away from home. I slept well my first night. We were up for exercise and drill the next morning at 6:00 A.M.. We had breakfast and more drilling. The bulk of our time was spent in preparation for shipment out to camp where basic training would begin.

Basic Training

Two days later we boarded a train headed for Fort Sill in Lawton, Oklahoma, where our basic training began. Upon arrival, I found that Fort Sill was very different from Fort Sam Houston. What struck me initially was that Fort Sill was much larger; however, it seemed that the only thing there to see were big guns. I found out later that it was, in fact, quite an intriguing place from a historical standpoint—the place where the American Indians struggled as a last stand to maintain their individual freedom and where heroes of that era, such as Geronimo, were made.

Our first day here we were assigned to barracks and divided into drill squads. The next morning we were divided into batteries of about ninety-six men each. There were five batteries: three firing batteries (A, B, C), a headquarters battery, and a service battery. The headquarters battery was the operational battery for the battalion, responsible for all record keeping and operations; the service battery kept lines of communication open between all five batteries and was responsible for supplying ammunition to the firing batteries; and the three firing batteries did the firing and carried the fight to the enemy during a battle. Each of the three firing batteries had four guns with a crew of about thirteen soldiers. Each crew had a chief of section, who held a buck sergeant rank; a gunner, usually holding corporal rank; and eleven cannoneers, who were privates and privates first class. A chief of the firing battery held staff sergeant rank and had overall responsibility for all twelve guns in three firing batteries. With this organizational structure, responsibilities could be assigned quickly to each soldier in the various crews, with measurable results.

Our training began with the nomenclature of the gun and its maintenance. At the time, the guns used consisted of 155-mm howitzers and 155-mm guns, called "Long Toms." The difference between howitzers and Long Toms was their firing trajectory. The howitzer had a rounded trajectory, and the Long Tom had flatter trajectory. This difference in trajectory seemed insignificant at first, but the difference would actually save my life later on in my army career.

We spent our first week on disassembling the breach of a 155-mm howitzer: taking it apart and reassembling it in a minimum of time while blindfold.

Artillery piece used for basic training: 155-mm howitzer; 6.1-inch caliber; 8,184 pounds; 95-pound shells; and a firing range of 16,000 yards.

The third day of disassembly, I incorrectly placed a key in the breach of the gun, and the sergeant singled me out for punishment. He attempted to humiliate me by having me scrub the concrete porch entry to our barracks with a toothbrush and to continue the cleaning while soldiers entered our barracks after training in the evening. I am not too sure about the merits of this type of punishment, but I gained a total respect for my gun and its maintenance.

By the end of the first week, the crews, while blindfold, were disassembling and reassembling the breach of the howitzer in record time. In our second week, we were taken out on the firing range to observe a gun crew firing a weapon. In this case, it was a Long Tom. Here we were taught how to squat and open our mouth to save our eardrums from being ruptured because of the gun's muzzle blast when it fired. Initially, I did not believe that our bodies physically could withstand repeated blasts from the muzzles of these large guns, but repeated use showed that they presented no problems.

The next five weeks were spent on the firing range. We started out firing directly at still targets and then switched to moving targets. "Enemy" tanks suddenly appeared in front of us, in some cases just when we were ready to fire. Another drill included being moved through a field and forced to dismount, set up, and fire while the enemy mortar and tanks were zeroing in on our position. I learned quickly that speed and accuracy in firing would save your life. The end of this cycle of basic training led to a final test, and I won the distinction of fastest, most accurate gunner in the 31st Battalion, which promoted me to corporal and a permanent gunner.

Next we moved on to the bivouac phase of our training. To initiate this phase, we shifted to the Wichita Mountains that surround Fort Sill. What first struck me about the Wichita Mountains was that it was very cold there at night, both in summer and winter. Here we were taught how to live outside and to fire on mountainous and military targets in small villages. An outstanding feature of this mountainous training came from learning to live with diamondback rattlesnakes. Because they are cold-blooded, they depended on exterior sources of heat to keep warm at night, so they would come and curl up against our tents in an effort to keep warm. The first thing we did every morning was walk around our tent looking for rattlesnakes. Since they never came inside, we learned to coexist. We never tried to kill them as long as they stopped at the door of our tents. We completed this, our bivouac phase, in about four weeks without incident.

During our last weeks of basic training, we sharpened up our drill skills and began discussing a new gun we were about to be introduced to—the 4.5-inch gun. It was a high-muzzle-velocity gun designed primarily for warfare in Germany, attacking pillboxes and stationary obstacles set up as part of the German Siegfried line, called the West Wall. We had to learn some new firing techniques because these guns fired a straighter trajectory than the curved trajectory of our howitzers. We quickly learned everything about these guns and got ready to put them on the firing line.

In 1939 the U.S. Army Ordnance Department designed two new pieces—a 4.7-inch gun and a 155-mm howitzer—both of which used the same carriage. It was later decided that the 4.7-inch gun would be changed to 4.5 inches to allow ammunition compatibility with our British allies. It was normally used for introduction or counterbattery fire. The 4.5-inch gun M1 was found to have exceptional range, capable of firing a fifty-five-pound projectile more than fifteen miles. However, the bursting capability of the projectile was inferior to the requirements of the day. At the close of World War II, the 4.5-inch gun M1 was withdrawn from service, and the 155-mm howitzer M1 took its place. The howitzer was more accurate and consistent at maximum range.

　　　　　　　　　　　　　　　　　　　　CHAPTER 2

Artillery piece used in advanced training and in combat: 4.5-inch gun (called 4.5s); 12,455 pounds; 55-pound shells; and a firing range of 25,715 yards.

The 31st Battalion

The composition of the 31st Battalion by educational status was some-what special. Half of the enlisted men had some college training in the ROTC from colleges with predominantly African American students, such as Prairie View A&M College, Texas College, Wiley College, and Bishop College. Other special enlisted men were recruited into the battalion, such as Ezzard Charles, who became world heavyweight boxing champion after the war. Most of these college-trained enlisted men came into the army as part of the Army Enlisted Reserve Corps training program. This meant that half of the 523 enlisted men in the battalion were considered the elite of the African American male population, both physically and in terms of education. This gave the battalion an excellent pool from which to select noncommissioned officers.

The lack of opportunity to become a commissioned field artillery officer became an issue with some of the noncommissioned officers, particularly those who had been high-ranking officers in the Prairie View ROTC. However, things were moving so quickly in our preparation for overseas duties that my interest in becoming an air artillery officer diminished. I became fascinated with learning the calculations for firing at targets by direct laying. I really wanted to be in a firing battery. I was promoted to the position of chief of section. We were issued new high-velocity 4.5-inch guns, which made the position more interesting. I later became chief of the firing battery, which placed me in charge of the four guns in Battery B.

The other half of the enlisted men in our battalion were high school graduates. They made good cannoneers because they quickly learned the strategies needed to fire big guns accurately.

All officers of the 31st Battalion were white, with the exception of one colored warrant officer stationed in the headquarters battery. The white officers were respectful toward the majority colored enlisted men, and they were rewarded for their efforts. The colored enlisted men supported their white officers. This accounted for the credit awarded the 31st Battalion as among the most efficient field artillery units to come through the training cycle at Fort Sill. Two highly respected officers of Battery B who stand out in my mind are First Lieutenant Yasco of the University of Illinois and First Lieutenant Smith of Texas A&M University.

At the termination of the war, my battalion was dismantled overseas. I lost contact with my commanders and the majority of the enlisted men. The few enlisted men I saw after the war had returned to Prairie View to complete their education.

After thirteen weeks, our basic training was complete, and we were ready to move on for advanced training. I was told we were going to California for the training. I received a ten-day pass so that I could go back home to visit parents and friends. I found all was well, but everyone was becoming increasingly concerned about the deaths being reported from the war zone and about the coming invasion of Europe. They knew that because of the type of training I received, I would be sent overseas as a participant soon. While visiting home, I found out that Clarence, my younger brother, had been inducted into the army while I was away. Now my mother and father had three sons in the army and all exposed to potential danger. Clarence was trained in army intelligence and had already been shipped to a post somewhere in the Philippines, and my older brother, Charles, had been in North Africa for more than a year.

While on furlough, I went to Prairie View to visit some friends and to see what campus life was like during wartime. I remember walking out of the administration building and seeing the campus chaplain, Rev. Lee C. Phillips, holding class in the middle of the campus with only female students surrounding him. As I walked toward the class, he came and met me and introduced me to his class. The female students greeted me one by one, and

I could see they were sad with all of the able-bodied male students gone. I spent part of the day on the campus before returning home. I found, while on campus and at home, that I too was changing, and my thoughts kept drifting back to camp, my training, and the mission I knew was soon in store for me. Back at home that same night, we all said good-bye and I rushed to catch the train to get back to camp. The conductor of the train saw me running toward it and literally stopped the train to allow me to get aboard. The rush made it easier to say good-bye to my mother, dad, and grandmother. I arrived back in camp at Fort Sill early the next morning.

On my return, most of the activity was spent preparing for shipment to our next camp for advanced training. My train ride to Fort Sill reminded me of earlier days when, as kids, we traveled by train to visit my grandfather, who lived on an apple farm just a few miles outside Muskogee, Oklahoma. Because my dad was a railroad laborer, we had free passes to travel on the MKT railroad. I was about nine or ten years of age when we last traveled to Muskogee, but my thoughts kept drifting back to earlier times. It was about daybreak when I arrived at the station in Lawton, Oklahoma. I caught a bus that took me about twenty miles to Fort Sill. The training at Fort Sill had been so intense that I found myself becoming attached to the post. I realized that much more had to be learned, so I had to keep moving. I was also excited about the new guns we would take into battle for the first time, and I was anxious to get them on the field to test my skills. We had been told earlier that they were designed for use in Germany and that we needed to know how to use them efficiently as support weapons. We began boarding the train the next morning for our new training site. The thirteen-week basic training at Fort Sill had gone quickly, and it was amazing to see how rapidly I had become attuned to the ways of army life and the use of our new guns.

Advanced Training

On August 13, 1943, the 31st Battalion of 523 African American enlisted men and 41 Anglo-American officers left Fort Sill, Oklahoma, by rail. The battalion arrived at Camp Beale, California, two days later. The 31st Battalion was relabeled at Camp Beale as the 777th Field Artillery Battalion, a label that stands today. The battalion was organized under the command of Lt. Col. Gilbert B. Lamb, but on November 17, 1943, Lt. Col. L. G. Witmer assumed command and remained throughout the duration of the activities and life of the 777th.

The training at Camp Beale somewhat duplicated our bivouac training at Fort Sill, just more intense. Day after day we sharpened our skills at attacking moving targets and firing at precision targets. We could disassemble and reassemble our guns in just a few minutes; we could be riding along a road in our tractor prime mover (the vehicle used to tow 4.5-inch guns), spot an enemy target, dismount, and have a round in the air in three minutes; we could fire one round at a distant target and have two other rounds on the way before the first round hit the target. We practiced our firing skills from dusk to dawn, day and night, rain or shine. In the midst of this firing, the importance of gun maintenance was constantly emphasized, in that if one misfired while facing an enemy, we could all be killed.

Two other Anglo-American artillery battalions were at Camp Beale, the 775th and the 776th. We had interbattalion competition in firing, loading, gun maintenance, and athletic competition, particularly boxing. This all took place toward the end of our training cycle. The 777th prevailed. During the time of this competition, I was promoted to chief of section, giving me my own gun with a crew of thirteen and a rank of sergeant. We completed our training about a year later and immediately began making preparations for overseas duty. We had trained and trained for months, so we were ready to go. You could feel it in the air; it was time to move to the last step, combat with the enemy. The median age for my crew was nineteen years, a stage where we felt that we could handle anything, especially after all of the physical and mental training we had just undergone. In the evenings, after training all day, I began to think more seriously about our upcoming mission and all that would have to be accomplished in enemy territory. We had been well prepared and indoctrinated in the fundamentals of field artillery warfare. Now it was time to put them to the test.

Passes to San Francisco

Before leaving for overseas shipment, my battalion was given passes to visit San Francisco, which was approximately 150 miles from our location. I had read so much about the state of California and the city of San Francisco in my geography class that I was eager to see it firsthand. This would be an expansion of what, up until now, was my exposure to a very limited geographic universe.

Two white battalions, the 775th and 776th, had received orders to leave Camp Beale with us, so they also were given passes to San Francisco. We always had good, clean competition with them during our military training in sports and on the firing range. We were acquainted with one another even though we had segregated facilities on the army base and did not socialize together. An army bus transported all three battalions to San Francisco.

We arrived to find the city enveloped in low fog, its skyscrapers seeming to float above it. Later in the day, buildings clustered on the hills glistened in the sunlight. I had never seen houses constructed on hillsides before, and I wondered about the expertise engineers had to use for this type of construction. I was enchanted with the beauty of the majestic city.

Even though the white and colored soldiers were assigned to separate groups, we were combined for many military activities. After arriving in San Francisco, we broke up into groups of four to six soldiers. I stayed with Sergeant Woods, one of our chiefs of section. Being older and having been in the army for many years, Sergeant Woods knew more about this town, as well as other cities, than all of us combined. We took a taxi to a big stately Victorian house on a hillside near the suburbs of the city. The entrance path leading up to the house took us past a verdant garden landscaped with lush foliage, overhanging vines with red blossoms, and the romantic, pungent fragrance of sweet olive. This house had the perfect exterior setting for an atmosphere of fun and relaxation. A proverb came to mind: "Behind mountains are more mountains." With the crew chief behind me, I walked onto the porch and rang the doorbell. No one responded. After the second ring a middle-aged lady appeared and escorted us to a large room, which she referred to as her den. About a dozen women and a few soldiers were standing around drinking cocktails and soft drinks. I realized right away that this was a house of prostitution. I recalled that during a conversation one night in camp, a soldier who had previously lived in San Francisco told us that such facilities were available and easily accessible.

The middle-aged woman who admitted us was the house madam. She introduced us to the women, who appeared to be between twenty and twenty-five years old. Half of them were white and half were colored, about the same racial proportion as the soldiers present. Soft music was playing. I observed that a soldier would select a girl and dance. During the dance the girl would make a sexual proposition, and the couple would leave the room.

I was slow in making my selection, as everything that was happening was new to me and to most of the other eighteen- and nineteen-year-old soldiers there. One pattern I quickly noticed was that the white soldiers were selecting colored girls and the colored soldiers were migrating more toward the white girls. This open selection process was a surprise to me, as I had never socialized with whites before. In general, I noticed there was a novelty appeal running both ways in the freelancing open environment.

An attractive young African American woman standing by a window caught my attention. I surmised that she was about twenty years of age. She had light brown skin and beautiful brown eyes. She appeared to be quieter and more sedate, as she sat apart from the rest of the group. When I walked over and asked her to dance, her face lit up in a broad smile. We danced to one of my favorite songs by the Ink Spots, "If I Didn't Care." After the dance ended, we retired to a bedroom. We sat down on a nineteenth-century bed with sheets that appeared to be silk. She proceeded to unbutton my GI shirt, which had large, difficult buttons. Then I unbuttoned her blouse and slipped it off. Her skin looked and felt too cared for and soft for her to be a prostitute.

My escort and I stood up beside the bed and continued to undress. Her perfect, alluring body was standing in front of me. This ritual was basically our only preparation, and we began lovemaking right away. It continued for some time, but she eventually said that it was time to finish up. At this point the door to the room opened. A man stood there gazing at us but did not utter one word. However, my escort commented to him that we were about to finish. He closed the door and walked away. That unexpected entry greatly diminished the pleasure of the experience for me from that point on.

Shortly thereafter, she helped me dress; then I kissed her on the cheek and told her how much I enjoyed the time I spent with her. She said that I was extra special and she wanted to see me again. I replied that I would try to return someday.

I discovered later that the house we visited was the home of the madam and that the women there were housewives who had husbands overseas. The man who came to the door was my young escort's husband. He permitted her to perform acts of prostitution to entice the other women to pursue this occupation as a pastime to alleviate their boredom, and for his financial gain. My initial impression of the women was that none of them truly fit the profile of a prostitute that I had envisioned.

Later on, our group of soldiers reassembled, returned to the downtown area, and spent the rest of the day sightseeing. We then enjoyed a delicious seafood dinner at a world-famous restaurant on Fisherman's Wharf.

Our last free day before going overseas went quickly. It felt good being able to clear my mind of the prospect of war and fighting for a day and just have fun. We boarded our bus and were back in camp by 7:30 P.M. I thought about the prostitute often that night before going to sleep, but the preparations for the long train ride across the country the next morning erased most memories of her. But this had been the first real sexual experience of my life, and it had a surprising sweetness for which I was unprepared. The next morning, August 2, 1944, we left for the port of embarkation for overseas duty.

CHAPTER 3

To the War in Europe

By August 1944, our training at Camp Beale was completed, so we were ready to move on. We packed our gear and boarded a train that transported us to an east coast port for embarkation for overseas duty. Our troop train left at sunrise. Just before boarding the train, I looked toward the east on my last early morning here at Beale and marveled at the sunrise. The morning, at the time of our departure, was misty; it looked as if we might get some rain later in the day. This was odd for that part of California, which has a desertlike climate and is virtually devoid of rain. I had been here for almost a year and found that the dry climate and open spaces reminded me somewhat of home. Marysville, the little town nearby that I occasionally visited, was a near replica of a small West Texas frontier town.

Our first day of travel was one of grandeur and admiration of the bounty and beauty of nature. The mountains and flowing valleys that we passed through could only have been created by a divine hand. The train stopped en route within just a few feet of the side of a mountain with exposed rock where we could see evidence of the rainfall and climate millions of years ago. I found this fascinating—I had never before seen anything like this scenery. I had been around railroads all my life, but I had never seen curves where the engine and the caboose are standing opposite each other going in different directions. "Nature is the living, visible garment of a cosmic deity and is man's best teacher." She unfolds her treasures to our search, unseals our eyes, illuminates our minds and purifies our hearts; an influence breathes from all the sights and sounds of her existence—she shows us only the surface of her inexhaustible wealth, but she is millions of fathoms deep.

On August 6, we finally arrived at Camp Myles Standish in Boston. We picked up final wares, got all of our legal and health papers in order, wrote letters home, and made all final plans before leaving the states. The long train ride almost kept us in a vacation frame of mind, but making last-minute preparations to embark into the unknown forced us to realize what we were about to engage in and our purpose for being here. As I looked around at our gun crews, they seemed a little more solemn now but still somewhat excited, with a visible seriousness of purpose in their eyes. Their facial expressions were relaxed and gave the appearance of readiness for the task ahead.

Crossing the Atlantic

On August 11, 1944, we completed all departure preparations at Camp Myles Standish and headed for the Boston port of embarkation, arriving in late evening. The weather was warm with a hazy overcast like it might rain later that night. Upon our arrival at the Boston port, we went directly to a waiting transport ship. In line to ascend the gangplank, I glanced up and the ship seemed very tall. The soldiers and sailors already aboard appeared to be far away.

My turn came to go up the gangplank, so I picked up my duffel bag, threw it across my back, and started upward. When I reached the top and stepped aboard, guides directed me to a deck below and to my assigned bed. The steel beds were very small-framed bunk beds stacked in rows. This arrangement allowed the maximum number of sleeping spaces for passing soldiers. My bed was the second bunk from the bottom, which made me feel safe from falling out during rough seas, as some of the bunks were quite high. It was about midnight by this time, and I decided to go up on deck just to see what things looked like. Our ship was moving slowly, alone in the water, with beacon lights nearby and at distances as far as the eye could see. I looked up, and there were large balloonlike objects just floating in the air all around us. This was a form of protection for our ship against enemy aircraft. The deck was crowded even though it was midnight, but all the soldiers were quiet. I looked beyond human-made objects in the sky and saw Orion's Belt hanging low in the western sky, which told me I had better get in bed if I wanted to get any sleep before sunrise. I took a minute before retiring to search the heavens for the North Star, referred to as the "Lone Star" in Texas, and could not find it. This told me that my geographic location had changed, and I was a long way from the space and the Lone Star above my beloved home in Texas.

The big ship sat steady almost without any movement, because the ocean was so calm. The surface seemed as slick as glass. It reminded me of Inks Lake located in the Hill Country of Texas where my family would go and launch our boat to spend the night. I fell asleep right away, as it had been a long day. About 6:00 A.M. I heard a buglelike sound announcing chow time. (I had become used to bugle sounds now, so there was no effect like the alarming sound my first night in the army.) After getting dressed, which was essentially washing up, as we slept in our green work fatigues, I went to the dining hall for breakfast. At breakfast, for the first time, I saw thousands of soldiers coming from all decks of the ship. I think there may have been ten thousand soldiers on our ship, more than I had ever seen at one time. The food was hot and good for a change; we were served bacon, eggs, grits, milk, juice, coffee, and a muffin. We had become accustomed to eating cold K rations (dried, packaged food) in the field. After breakfast, I went to the top deck again and looked around.

The days crossing the Atlantic were free days, as there was nothing to do except sail and wait. It was about 6:45, just at daybreak, when I stepped on the top deck and looked around at the various horizons. The scene was almost frightening. During the night, our ship had joined a convoy, and there were ships everywhere, as far as the eye could see, in all directions. These were other transport ships, ships resembling tankers, and on the outer perimeters, warships patrolling. I was told that these convoys covered an area of thirty miles, and they combined to avoid German submarine wolf-pack attacks. When I checked the same evening just before sunset, it seemed we were heading in a different direction if we used the sun itself as a base point. I learned that convoys follow a zigzag course, attempting to keep submarine wolf packs off balance. I was also told that not a single transport ship, transporting troops in convoys, had been sunk by a submarine since the beginning of the war.

Our first day at sea had been a beautiful day with just a slight mist falling during the early part of the morning. That night the skies were clear, making it almost possible to see with the naked eye beyond our solar system. The world seemed bigger in the middle of the ocean. In trying to describe the beauty of my first night at sea, out away from the lights and environmental contaminants of the cities, my mind kept drifting back to Shakespeare: "How absolute and omnipotent is the silence of the night and yet the stillness seems almost audible."

During the night coming into our second day at sea, the ocean turned rough and almost stormy. Before dawn I was thrown partly out of bed. But worst of all, about half the soldiers on our ship became seasick and missed breakfast. About 10:00 A.M. on our third day at sea, the water became calm and the sun shone bright as if the storm had never happened. Out on the ocean where the water was deep blue and peaceful, my mind drifted back to times of serenity and calmness. When day ends at sea, it appears that darkness just falls from the wings of night like a huge blanket.

CHAPTER 3

Early morning on our fourth day at sea, I saw a few duffel bags floating around along the ocean surface. They were at a distance and were half submerged as the wake of our ship kept pushing them along. I did not know what they were at first, but I soon recognized they were the same as my duffel bag and were still filled to capacity. Over to the left I saw three corpses floating face up, still wearing the same green fatigue army work uniform as I was wearing. The ship they were aboard had moved too far ahead of the convoy and had suffered a submarine attack. The cold, salty ocean water had washed their faces and army uniforms sparkling clean. It was very strange, but they looked alive just floating in the ice-cold ocean water, seemingly aware that their duffel bags were nearby within reaching distance. This scene was my first full awakening to the meaning of life and death, that death could overtake you right out here in the middle of the ocean. Our convoy kept its course and eventually pulled away from the drowned soldiers. I kept looking in their direction, but they just disappeared from view. The ocean waves began to consume them. They had looked alive. These lines from Alfred, Lord Tennyson's "Crossing of the Bar" kept haunting me:

> *But such a tide as moving seems asleep*
> *Too full for sound and foam*
> *When that which drew from out the boundless deep*
> *Turns again home.*

The ocean was trying to give up its dead. This also told me that in the recent past, a ship had been penetrated by enemy submarine packs and lives were lost. This was a constant reminder of the danger we faced on this joyride and cautioned me to keep focused on why I was there. The balance of my ten-day ocean crossing was uneventful. I became accustomed to seeing the sun rise and set in the ocean to the front and in the rear of us. I kept seeing rainbows. One evening I thought our ship was about to sail into the end of a rainbow and I could collect the pot of gold, as the legend goes, but it all just disappeared right before my eyes. In the early morning, just before sunrise on August 22, 1944, our convoy arrived at the port of Liverpool, England. Our journey across the Atlantic had been successful. Before us, one of our ships was lost to enemy submarine attacks and likely had drifted out of the cover of a convoy. The success of the first leg of my journey was a good omen for me.

So This Is England

The strange thing about our arrival in Liverpool was that there were no lights on in the city. It was completely dark. This was our first introduction to wartime conditions, where blackouts were maintained as a protection against exposing bombing targets to the enemy. We disembarked and were loaded on trucks waiting to transport us to army barracks for one night. On the morning of August 23, we mounted on trucks again and headed for Barnstaple, arriving the same day. Here we received all of our equipment and supplies, including our 4.5-inch guns, tractor prime movers, ammunition, communication equipment, and all the necessary secondary supplies.

Our supplies included winter clothes, our small arms, carbine rifles, and ammunition. On the morning of August 24, we left Barnstaple fully equipped, arriving at Nine Yews later in the day. Here we spent a few days fine-tuning our communication and firing skills before entering the battle zone. A light mist fell during the morning, with a pleasant seventy-degree temperature.

We had our first experience in a friendly foreign country, which included some of the racism that some American white soldiers transported across the seas and gave to the local population. Nine Yews had coal mines. After a day of field artillery activity, my battalion used the coal miners' bath facilities, where three hundred to four hundred soldiers could shower at one time. Nine Yews was subject to the same blackout rules as all other cities and towns in England. This meant there were blackout cloths over all windows in the shower facilities. One night while showering, a soldier observed that one window was not completely blacked out and told the soldier nearest the window to pull the blackout cloth over farther to cover the entire window. He walked over to the window, but before he began to pull the cloth over, he looked out. What he saw was a shock. Outside, hundreds of English people, men and women, were taking turns looking at us shower. They were looking primarily for the "tails" that the white American soldiers had told them we had. After this experience the whole concept backfired on the white soldiers because the English people took a special liking to the African American soldiers, who they found to be caring and gentle. Some of the white American soldiers carried that same "tail" concept all over Europe, but it backfired on them in Europe as it did in most of the world. We had military authority but treated all people with respect, and the Europeans responded to this. Our short stay in England was a pleasant one and a rich experience. In those few days, we had closer and warmer contact with white people in a social gathering for soldiers than we had ever experienced in our own country.

A recreation center run by British civilians was open for troops in the Nine Yews area. They sent out special invitations inviting troops of the 777th Field Artillery to the USO-type activities, including dances. It was amazing to observe how much at ease the British women seemed to be socializing and dancing with African American troops. The 777th Field Artillery had just two nights to enjoy the British hospitality. I met "Lina" the one night I attended activities at the recreation center. This setting was a totally new experience for me, for I had had no social relation with white people. As I walked into the center, an attractive young lady stood just a few paces left of the door. I walked over and asked her for a dance. She accepted and wanted to know right away where I was from and how long had I been in England. We had a lively discussion extending even after the dance was over. I finally let her know we were leaving the next day. I kept saying I hoped to see her again sometime in the future. She was my first experience dancing and holding conversation with a white girl. She was a delight. I was always curious to know what they wanted to talk about on a one-on-one basis. What I discovered was that it is all about the ordinary. About 11:00 P.M. I went over to Lina to say goodnight and good-bye. She followed me out to our waiting bus, where I told her spending the evening here and the time with her had been a real pleasure. It had been so long since I had talked to anyone in a social setting.

For the purpose of moving to a channel port en route to the continent of Europe, we left Nine Yews on September 14, arriving at a staging area, sub-area D-6 England, the same day, covering a distance of twenty-five miles. The condition of the roads was good, and the weather clear and sunny. The face of the war had scarcely surfaced in these small English villages, in contrast with the destruction we witnessed in Liverpool and as we passed through the larger cities. In fact, there was almost a sense of peacefulness until you looked up and saw planes returning from bombing runs in Germany, some damaged, and one even falling from the sky as it tried to make it home.

On to Bricquebosq, France

On September 16, we departed from the staging area and moved to Portland Harbor, where our entire battalion, complete with all equipment and personnel, was loaded on two LSTs (Landing Ship-Tank) for the ten-mile trip across the English Channel. At the beginning of this sail, the weather was cloudy and the rain was falling steadily. However, shortly after we set sail, the weather cleared and the sun made its appearance. As we approached Utah Beach on the French coast the evening of September 16, my first observation was the violent destruction of equipment and lives that had taken place here just a few months earlier at the time of the D-day invasion on June 6. Mangled and burned-out equipment still permeated the beach landscape. I passed a tree a few hundred yards inland from the beach where a young American paratrooper was lodged after he dropped behind the German lines on the morning of the invasion. He was carrying equipment on his back that was heavier than his body weight. He was left in the tree half the morning of June 6 before our forces could dislodge and rescue his dead body for burial. This incident was recorded in the June 1944 issue of *Stars and Stripes.*

Our next motor march occurred after we debarked from the two LSTs at Utah Beach. Here, we were situated in area 18 and remained at this location from my birthday, September 17, to September 21. On the afternoon of September 21, we departed for Bricquebosq, France, arriving there on the same day, covering a distance of about forty miles. The weather was clear and dry, but the roads for this drive were in poor condition, largely as a result of the frequent shelling that took place in this area during heavy fighting in the battles of the hedgerows. In France, small farms were not fenced off as they were in the United States but were separated by five- to six-foot mounds around the perimeter of the farms called hedgerows. Many of these small farms had become battlefields because the hedgerows shielded enemy tanks. Bricquebosq was a temporary station for us for a few weeks. On September 25, two of our officers and seventy-six cannoneers left the battalion on detached service with the Ninth Army on a secret destination. These officers and enlisted men took with them thirty-six vehicles, which formed a portion of a truck convoy under the commanding officer of another field artillery battalion. This convoy served the purpose of transporting men and supplies to the front. The officers and enlisted men returned on October 6, minus one vehicle, which had been wrecked. On this special assignment our trucks covered a distance of about twenty-one hundred miles. No other motor marches were undertaken until October 25, at which time we began our movement up to the front.

The Accident

On October 15, we were still at Bricquebosq. It was raining the morning we advanced and secured new positions. We opened the trails (used to tow the gun and prevent it from shifting after firing) on gun number 3, Battery B, and fired a round adjusting our field of fire using supercharged powder base. Due to the softness of the ground, the left trail kicked out of the ground and closed in on me, striking my left knee and stretching it inward all the way to the ground. When the trail was removed, I could not walk and was rushed to one of our field hospitals a few miles away.

The field hospital complex was composed of a series of tents converted into a hospital with several wings large enough to accommodate about 750 wounded and injured soldiers. The ward I was assigned to gave medical aid to the injured and those wounded from small-arms fire and artillery explosions. Double-deck steel beds lined the walls of both sides of the hospital wings. I was in the lower-deck bed, number 25, on the east wall. A team of doctors would make rounds each morning, reading charts and checking the condition of each soldier. During these rounds, they made decisions about whether the soldier should remain here for treatment or be discharged to other facilities. Most of the patients were white soldiers, because white soldiers made up the bulk of combat units in the European theater of operations, where the likelihood of wounds or injuries was increased.

According to the army's racist policies, most colored soldiers were relegated to service units, such as the Quartermaster Corps, where the likelihood of injury was minimized. Another colored soldier was on my wing of the

Evacuation hospital in Normandy, France.

hospital in bed 11. He was part of an antiaircraft unit that came ashore on D-day. His left leg was blown off above the knee from a mortar shell, and part of his stomach was actually open. About 250 wounded white soldiers were on this wing. An incident occurred as a team of doctors made their rounds one morning. As the leader of the team approached the colored soldier in bed number 11, he paused and then asked the soldier, "Boy, what are you doing here?" Total silence fell over the entire ward. Soldiers ceased talking immediately, with astonished looks on their faces.

The voice of the colored soldier was impaired; he could scarcely speak. He was stunned at the doctor's comment but did not say anything. The white soldier in the next bed had neck and shoulder wounds. You could hardly see his face for his bandages, but he was outraged by the doctor's question. He rose up in his bed, faced the lead doctor, and yelled out to him, "He's here to see your mama!" The doctor hesitated and then immediately turned to face his team to observe their reactions to the white soldier's response on behalf of the colored soldier. He abruptly turned and walked away without speaking, his team following behind him. Later that morning, some of the members of his team returned to the ward with another lead doctor. I never saw the original lead doctor again. The point here is that even though this white lead team doctor was a racist, the white wounded enlisted man spoke out against his racist attitude in the strongest language. I learned it was risky to paint all whites with the same brush with reference to racial attitudes.

I was diagnosed with severe stretched ligaments in my left knee. Fluids accumulated under my kneecap, which restricted my mobility. Heat treatments were administered daily for the first few days. The doctors kept me there a week and concluded that the facilities were not adequate to treat my knee because it was so badly damaged. I was to be sent back to England or even the States for treatment. By that afternoon, September 26, I was on a hospital LST headed back to England.

The hospital ship was white with a large Red Cross sign across the top. There was no effort to conceal the presence of the ship, I suppose because of its hospital status. Stretchers and gurneys were brought ashore, and loading began about 2:00 P.M. We set sail across the English Channel about 8:30. The ship was filled to capacity with the injured, wounded, and dying. Everything was so still that you could hear only the lap of the water as the ship steered its way out into the channel.

I was nineteen years old; the other wounded soldiers looked even younger. A young, blond white boy on the bunk to my left had a gravel sound in his voice as he tried to talk, but no visible wounds. My attention was attracted

CHAPTER 3

by a nurse bringing pain pills, and when I looked over to hear the balance of the young soldier's conversation, he was dead, just that quick. He appeared to have been about seventeen or eighteen. Some had severe wounds—their faces were bandaged, but part of the face was gone—still they were quiet. You knew they were dead when you did not see any movement. One young soldier in a bed in front of me got up off his bed, walked to the end, turned around to lie down, and fell over dead. He had not a single visible scar on him. I discovered that many of the soldiers who died like that had internal injuries from artillery mortar or bomb blasts. We were on a mercy ship, but a better name was a floating hearse because so many of these young, wounded soldiers died in transit.

These scenes made a big impact on me. I kept thinking that the young soldiers, all about my age, had put themselves to the test and paid a high price for doing so. And here I was, one of the best-trained artillerymen in the army, about to go home without even facing the test. I kept thinking about the months and months of intensive training and my gun crew who would soon have to face the enemy without my presence. I considered all of this unacceptable.

We landed just before sunrise on the morning of September 27. Trained medics took the injured, the wounded, and the dead to designated stations. I was assigned to a British hospital and to a British medical officer who was waiting to make an evaluation of my physical status and a determination of my final outcome: treatment and assignment to a noncombat unit or home to the States. The theory was that since I would not have full mobility in Germany, the risk of my being killed was too high. Instead, I could perform valuable services in less risky areas. It appears that my battalion commander had communicated my importance to the unit as a gun commander (chief of section), as they had me first on the list to evaluate.

As soon as I was taken to the hospital, I found the head of the medical team's office and went directly there, dressed in the army pajama suit I received upon boarding the hospital ship in France. I found his office and knocked on the door. I heard muffled talking, and someone asked, "Who is it?" I walked in and identified myself. Six doctors sat around a table reviewing the cases they were to evaluate. My folder was on top. They asked me why I was there. I told them my story, what I had seen on the ship, and explained the bond between myself and my crew who were about to go into Germany, and that I understood clearly the wide difference between what we call true courage and a mere contempt of life. Finally, I told them I felt I could handle myself and wanted to go back to my unit immediately. They took me to an adjoining room and asked me to lie down on a table. They examined the reflex of my knee and whether or not fluid was accumulating under my kneecap. After the examination, I was asked to go to a waiting room three doors down the hall. Two hours later, a nurse took me back to the examining room. The head physician then told me of the adversities I could encounter resulting from the fluids accumulating under my kneecap. They explained especially how the coldest winter they were experiencing in Europe could impact my mobility, particularly by my having to live outside in the cold. I was given the option, by the team of British doctors, to remain in the hospital for three or four weeks for treatment and observation or to go back to my unit immediately and take my chances. Without hesitation, I took the option to return to Europe immediately and accepted the risk. The head physician signed my release papers and papers for a ticket as a passenger on the LST crossing the channel that afternoon. I stood up, and each of the six doctors shook my hand and said, "Sergeant Owens, good luck Ole Chappie." I thanked them, took my release papers, and boarded a waiting bus to take us to the port. I left England at 4:30 P.M. on September 27, 1944.

The group of soldiers on the bus was different from the group I came over with the previous night. These were their replacements, some brand-new, right from the States, and some a little older who had been wounded or hurt and were returning to battle. When I make reference to older, I am referring to twenty- or twenty-two-year-olds. War takes its toll on individuals, making them look and act older. The older group of soldiers were usually quiet and somber, whereas the really young, clean-faced ones were somewhat jolly, not really comprehending the danger that lay ahead. They looked so young. I kept thinking about the little, blond boy who died so quickly last night without a whisper and the youngster who got up and walked a few steps, looking perfectly healthy, and just died trying to lie down. It was now about 2:30 in the afternoon. The same schedule as yesterday. We set sail for Normandy (Utah Beach).

The ride seemed so peaceful this time. No one would have believed there were a thousand ships in these waters just three months ago; on this day we were all alone. This seemed like a joyride. What was missing was the dress attire. The code of dress consisted of combat boots, green fatigues, steel helmets, and rifles or carbines. The mission here was different—to kill or be killed. As we got near the beach where land was visible, the mood among the young soldiers changed—they became quieter and more somber.

It was a cool day and an even cooler night. We docked about 7:30, and buses were waiting to carry us to the train station, where we would be transported to the vicinity of our units. The various units were in great need of replacements, so the army had an efficient system of getting replacements to the right place fairly quickly. During the ten days I was away from my unit, they had begun preparing to move north to the front. Once the Germans retreated from the fighting in the hedgerows and the city of Saint Lô, France, fell, they retreated rapidly north to the Siegfried line surrounding the western part of Germany. This was where they would make their stand, and my battalion was trained primarily to participate in this conflict. Our new 4.5-inch high-velocity guns were designed mainly for penetrating German defenses by destroying concrete bunkers.

The buses dropped us off at the train station. The waiting trains were really boxcars. I remember seeing the sign on each boxcar—"8 chevaux ou 40 hommes"—meaning each car would hold eight horses or forty men. The trains seemed small compared to those I had helped my dad work on at home, but they were very fast. We had been issued K rations, which we ate as we rode on the train.

When the train stopped in a small town to refuel, I heard a soldier yell, "Sergeant, there he is!" I looked up and saw a German V-1 rocket with its engine cut off gliding down toward the train. It appears the rocket launchers were waiting for the arrival of the train. The rocket fell short, hitting the tracks behind the train, damaging the tracks and the rear boxcar. All of the soldiers evacuated the car after the impact. We had been told if a buzz bomb flies over and you can hear it, everything is all right, because it has passed you. But if the engine cuts off, scout for cover, because it will be coming down somewhere near you. We all boarded the train again and continued our course. We rode all night. With the war in high gear, the forward progress of the train was slow, with frequent stops to try to avoid air attacks. We arrived in Bricquebosq at sunrise on September 28. Army buses waited to take us to our various units. My unit was on standby, waiting for the next move to Germany and the front lines.

March to the German Front

On October 25, 1944, we were preparing to pull out of our safe-haven, rear-echelon position at Bricquebosq with strict regulations. Front-line elements of our Ninth Army already were engaged in the great Allied push into the German heartland. Our time had come to move forward and support them in battle. As we packed our gear and loaded onto our tractor prime mover pulling our guns, I felt anxiety and seriousness of purpose. This was what we had prepared for so long and so hard.

I noticed that my crew members were all looking somber but carrying out their duties professionally, as they had been trained to do. They all seemingly slept well in anticipation of our march, which might require four days and nights in transit without sleep. The impact of our bivouac training at Fort Sill had taken its toll on us in terms of elevated confidence in our weapons and our capacity to cope with defensive ploys engaged in by the Germans. Nobody was overanxious to engage in combat to kill, but that is what we had been trained to do, and we accepted this risk. At sunset the previous evening, just as the sun neared the lower horizon, a flash of crimson splendor with blazing scarlet clouds appeared, which seemed to foretell impending weather for our coming march.

It was a gray morning. Gusts of stinging rain made us thankful for our waterproof combat jackets. However, the heavy rain failed to discourage the ever-present civilian camp followers, who came to combine their farewell with a final plea for the food ration we might leave with them. Everywhere undernourished and undersized French children crowded around our artillerymen. The adults, who were more reserved, lingered at a convenient distance, in the background. The children stepped up unobserved and tugged patiently at the side of each standing soldier, asking for rations for the baby or a "cigarette for Daddy." Finally, our battalion commander gave orders for us to break camp. As the long column of tractor prime movers and artillery guns rolled out through the town, young and old folks crowded the street, waving good-bye. After five years under the occupation of the Germans, the local French citizens had a great respect for the African American artilleryman.

Gun Crew.
Source: Pictoral Records
Center for Military
History, Washington,
D.C., 1951, 193.

The figure above shows the gun crew towing a column of 155-mm guns. The crew rides on the M3 tractor prime mover. My gun, the 4.5-inch, used a similar M1 tractor prime mover instead of the M3. The mode of towing was the same.

On our first day we traveled for hours through miles of French countryside. It was so tranquil with fall plowing and farm preparations that only the presence of the gun crew members at my side and the big guns we were propelling reminded me that we were headed to the front. Many of the black furrowed fields we passed and the long green valleys seemed very familiar to me, as if they had been plucked from around the Hill Country at home in Central Texas and just relocated in this spot. As we passed through the narrow streets of the storybook small towns, the people watched us with curiosity and a friendly interest. They seemed amazed at the massiveness of new war materials and fresh faces headed to the front. Some ran along beside our tractor and gave us food and home-cooked pies as we lumbered along their streets. We waved and gave gestures of thanks but could not consume the goodwill food and pie. It was against regulations, and there were other risks. The young women in the crowd stood silent and smiling, while the young children waved. One ran beside our slow-moving tractor and gave me flowers.

We traveled all day and finally reached Le Mans, France, at nightfall on October 26. We covered 150 miles this first day. After a few hours for refueling and walking around briefly for exercise in Le Mans, we headed for Paris. The rain had stopped by this time, and the skies changed from a dull gray to a metallic blue.

So That's Paris, France—at a Distance

On our second day the roads for our drive were full of potholes from shelling that took place in this area a few weeks ago. As we rolled along, I noticed that the landscape of the countryside was changing—more hills and long, narrow valleys. I saw workers tending vineyards for miles all along the roads as we passed through. The individual grapevines were laid out in perfectly straight rows—so straight they appeared to have been positioned by nature's divine hand. I have never witnessed such massive growing and harvesting of grapes for commerce. The smell of pesticides was still in the air from the spray used to protect the fruit against insects, pests, and diseases. As we passed through, seeing these vineyards for a brief moment, I found my mind drifting away from the prospect of armed conflict to that of growing and harvesting nature's productive output. I was reminded of my peach and plum research projects as a student at Prairie View. It was a good feeling.

On October 27 dusk found us approaching Paris. We drove all day at a slightly higher speed than usual. We bypassed the Paris city limits and headed north. In spite of my not entering Paris, there was a sense of excitement over being that close to a city I had read so much about when I was in high school. Once when I was in a school play, I had to repeat the phrase, "London is a man's town with power in the air; Paris is a woman's town with flowers in her hair." I could see and feel the daintiness of Paris at a distance while riding on a vehicle of war. We got close enough to the city limits to see the bright lights and hear the movement of the city.

Our column covered about 160 miles on this day. The skies were clear and blue, but the temperature was falling rapidly. The roads were gravel. Before our arrival, the city of Paris was believed to have been protected by a powerful German garrison. Therefore, we decided to bypass the city altogether and continue the main drive north.

On to Hirsen, France

We continued our northern journey all night. We slept well to the lulling rhythm of our tractor's steel treads as they plowed into the asphalt roads. This sound, along with the roar of our tractor engine, was all we could hear during the night, when there was scarcely any traffic on the road. Daybreak arrived, and I could see the sun trying to break through the eastern horizon. It was October 28, and we were approaching Hirsen, France. With the exception of a short break on the outskirts of Paris, we covered 150 miles during this stretch of our march. A haze covered the sky along with intermittent rain during the night. After we headed north from Paris, the weather changed and the temperature fell rapidly. It was predicted that Europe and Germany would encounter the coldest winter in one hundred years. Unfortunately, this prediction came true.

The roads here showed the results of the weeks of bombing and shelling. But in spite of the light rains and increasingly cold temperatures, people still congregated on the streets in the towns and villages. Some stared silently as we rumbled our big guns through their town. A few kids ran alongside our slow-moving convoy. From general observation, the people looked, spoke, and reacted differently in this part of France compared with those in the Utah Beach area. Their expressions were more reserved, and they showed fewer emotions. I suppose it is like back home in the United States, where appearance and language differences exist between Northern and Southern households. Upon arrival in Hirsen, at about 5:30 A.M., we dismounted, walked around, and refueled our tractor. By 7:30 we had completed our tasks, so we mounted and began the run to our final staging area before entering Germany.

The skies were clear with bright sunshine, but the temperature was steadily and rapidly falling. The air was crisp, and the cold began to penetrate our waterproof combat jackets. There was no rain in sight. The roads were in fair condition. We neared our final destination, Germany. Everything around us, the houses, streets, and fields, had been impacted by the war. We were beginning to miss our crowds on the streets as we passed through, and we noted a change in attitude and friendliness among the people, even though they were also French citizens. The fear in the air was simply pervasive.

To Tongeren, Belgium

After leaving Hirsen early in the morning, I watched convoys of empty trucks speed past our slow-moving column bound for the front lines in

Germany. Trucks headed toward the front were usually thought of as supply trucks delivering primarily ammunition and wares needed for combat missions. Late afternoon approached, and we began to meet the same trucks returning from the front lines, each cramped with newly captured German prisoners. Most were wearing caps instead of steel helmets, and they look tired, unshaven, dirty, and bare—the telltale signs of having been engaged in a near-death struggle. The prisoners were packed closely together in a standing position as they swayed slightly, jostling each other with the motion of the trucks. They eyed us and stared at our column, noticing the direction we were headed as they sped by, but their faces were devoid of expression. This was my first view of the German soldier other than pictures we had been shown in training back at Fort Sill. They carried an air of arrogance in spite of being caged on a 6x6 truck and defeated as prisoners of war. For them the war was over, and they appeared neither happy nor sad as they flashed by and were swallowed up in the growing darkness.

Night found us about twenty-five miles from our staging destination of Tongeren, Belgium. We reached this point just before midnight on October 29. Our march from the Normandy coast at Utah Beach covered a distance of about 600 miles, with the average length of our daily march 150 miles. The weather was variable throughout our march—damp and cloudy at the beginning of our journey and interspersed with frequent rain showers. On our third and fourth days, the weather became clear and dry but began turning cold. One night I even thought I was shivering from being wet and cold on an open moving tractor, but it turned out to be a quivering from the movement of my tractors' cleats smashing on a concrete surface as we moved along. My body would keep this motion awhile after my dismount. We had to steer the tractor more carefully now, as the roads were showing more signs of a war in progress.

We remained in Tongeren for three days, refueling, checking equipment and supplies, and getting a full night's rest after four days and nights in transit. I wrote letters home, telling my mother, dad, and grandmother that I was on the move but I could not say where, as I did not really know. I told them the vista through which I viewed the world when I saw them last had changed and was transformed into something that was completely off my map of understanding. I assured them that I was all right. I told them that I would describe my location in my next letter. It took me a full night to adjust fully to my body not quivering as my tractor rolled along.

Tongeren was almost like a vacation spot. Everything was so convenient. I experienced my first hot shower since we left the coal mines in England.

CHAPTER 4

Showers were private here. There were no onlookers checking to see if we had tails. Sleeping inside a house seemed very strange to me. Our helmets had been our washbasins. Our battalion began the day by watching a series of army-oriented movies, two in particular that tended to sharpen our focus on our purpose for being in active combat. Our attention was focused on what was required of each of us to try to stay alive. We had seen these same two movies more than a year ago while in advanced training at Camp Beale, California. The first film was *Kill or Be Killed*, and the second was *A Baptism of Fire*. Both movies showed soldiers under the stress of combat conditions and how different soldiers react to various levels of stress. It was so amazing to see that some soldiers kept their prior training in focus and adjusted quickly to combat adversities, while others fell apart when confronted by the enemy.

I remember discussing the *Kill or Be Killed* movie with the psychiatrist who was part of the team presenting the films. I asked him about the terms used in the film: *superego, ego,* and *id.* He said that the recruit's superego would tell him it was his duty to fight when faced by the enemy; his ego would convince him that fighting in the present circumstances was a good idea; and his id would arouse his emotions, fears, and anger. The psychiatrist pointed out that the films were necessary and important for our adjustment. The problem faced in performing duties was that the military wisdom of the day held that normal soldiers did not break down under the initial and sustained pressure from "a baptism of fire"; only neurotics did. This belief had led to a policy of screening "weaklings" out of the army at induction centers. The policy soon proved a failure, as psychiatric cases accounted for a high percentage of our casualties during the first week of engagements and for more than a third of all casualties being shipped home from the war, despite the fact that 12 percent of all men rejected at induction stations were turned down because of psychiatric reasons.

After the movies and discussions, we had the rest of the day off. We were leaving for our first engagement the next morning. A few men wrote letters, but most spent their time cleaning their carbines and sidearms. The majority slept—we all needed sleep after essentially being up for four days and nights in a row. Jack, my tractor driver, spent a lot of time cleaning the engine of his tractor. I had never seen him engage in a task with such concentration. The night air was crisp and cold, just the right component for soldiers needing a good night's rest.

In advanced training at Camp Beale, I had a policy of meeting with my crew weekly, usually toward the weekend, to discuss the training activities for the week and then anything that crew members wanted to talk about. Their personal discussion centered on problems with getting mail from home and regulations regarding weekend leave off the post. We usually had free-flowing discussions. We had our final crew-expression meeting at about 8:30 P.M. I opened by telling them tomorrow would be a new experience for us, but it was what we had trained for. We might run into circumstances that we had not seen before, but the American soldier is known to be resourceful and to make adjustments quickly when needed. I then gave each cannoneer five minutes to say anything he wanted, including raising any questions. We had not had a talk of this nature since we left Camp Beale, so it was time.

"Rainey" wanted his parents to know "your son will be locked in battle with the Germans tomorrow morning. You never believed your little boy right off the farm in Mississippi was capable." "Broodnact" wanted his mother to know "by daylight in the morning, your little boy will be engaged in battle with the flower of the German army; can you believe that? We've trained so we're ready." "Frazier" said, "They tell me our guns will hit a target fourteen miles and will go right through the fortifications in the Siegfried line; I will test it in the morning." "Fry" wanted to represent the foot soldier in final settlement of a defeated Germany. "Randle": "What do you train for? Let's get it on!"

"Norris" wanted his sister back in Fairfield, Texas, to know that he's in Germany and just entered the Siegfried line and is ready to carry it to the Germans. He wrote his mother that in the "twenty-four hours he has been in Germany, he has seen so much death and dying that he fears for his own life." "Napper" wanted his sister to know this is a dangerous place. "I just received a letter from Mama telling me my friend Richard left the United States in early 1943 bright-eyed and patriotic with all sorts of dreams for the future. He returned home a few months ago in 1944 as a mental patient."

"Evans": "I keep thinking about a duel point-blank with a mammoth German heavy tank and mobile artillery in a death struggle, where you kill or be killed. One miss of an approaching target almost always meant sudden death for defending cannoneers. We can't miss." "Burton": "Explosions and heavy gunfire thundered in the road leading to our gun position last night and early this morning. Tracer fire lit up the sky, enemy planes crisscrossed the battlefield, and one of our guns in Battery C was struck and put out of action. Of that gun crew, I'm not sure what happened to the cannoneers. And here we are at war—let's take it to them." "Hickman" said, "I've heard so much talk about the devastation that can be inflicted by their eighty-eight-millimeter guns. Let's see what the Germans will say tomorrow about our four-point-fives." "Stewart": "Here it's like a bivouac we experienced in the Wichita Mountains of Fort Sill—we blew up enemy targets approaching us there, as we will German Tiger tanks tomorrow." "Jack" said, "I want to tell my kids one day that I saw the horrors and fears of a war through my own eyes. I was a miserable, dirty, frightened half-frozen character."

I told them they were a good gun crew. There was a mist, but I thought tomorrow would be a good day—visibility should be good. "Everybody get a good night's rest."

To Richterich, Germany

I awakened early the morning of November 2, because I knew we were to continue our march today. The fact was that I was rested with only about three hours of sleep. I kept thinking all during the night about our movement into Germany the next morning. As I looked at the western horizon about midnight, I did not see Orion's Belt; instead, I saw the horizon light up as if it were daylight. I then realized that over there, a few hundred yards ahead of us, the black soil was Germany, where a war was in progress. We loaded our gear on the tractor before retiring. When I went out to make a final check at daylight, I was pleasantly surprised to find everybody already aboard our tractor and ready to go.

On November 2 at 9:00 A.M., our column left Tongeren on a march to occupy a combat position in Germany that had been selected previously. As we left Belgium, the intensity and frequency of the earth's vibrations I felt last night and the brightness of the lights flashing increased, telling me that we were not that far away from the combat zone. The separation between night and day disappeared as quickly as the twinkling of an eye.

The muzzle blast of so many artillery pieces firing simultaneously gave the impression that night was day. Long sleepless periods can cause confusion within the body's internal clock, throwing its timing and reasoning mechanisms completely out of focus. This is similar to photoperiodism in plants, in which artificial light can change the plant's night mode to a daylight mode. This can be beneficial. I recalled riding along stretches of highway in southern Florida where sugarcane was grown on both sides of the roads. There was a steep curve in one section of the highway. The plants in the cane field beyond the curve grew taller than cane plants growing along the straightaway because of the headlights of the cars that traveled on the highway. The artificial light from the cars caused the nighttime growth cycle of the plants to shift to a daytime growth cycle; therefore, the plants grew both day and night. The downside of this artificial stimulation is that the plants can be forced to never bear fruit and literally can grow themselves to death. It can cause the same disorientation and confusion in soldiers.

A defense barrier for western Germany, called the Siegfried line or the Western Wall, extended from the Netherlands to Switzerland. Human-made obstacles such as the "dragon teeth" were integrated carefully into the defense system of the line. The Siegfried line consisted of hundreds of pillboxes with interlocking fields of fire supported by an extensive system of command posts, observation posts, and troop shelters. Hitler's plan was for the Siegfried line to slow down an enemy invasion long enough for his troops to regroup and mount major counteroffensives. Any march from this position forward had the purpose of improving our position for combat readiness, for support, or for participation in newly initiated engagements where success depended on the adequacy of artillery backup.

As our column lumbered along, I looked out over a small crest and saw "dragon teeth" directly in front of my tractor at the start of the outer rim of the Siegfried line. This was so sudden that it took me by surprise. It was a little scary to realize I was actually sitting up in the middle of the German Siegfried line that we had studied and read about so often in advanced training.

We had been shown movies about the "dragon teeth" and trained on how they could be destroyed. They were designed to keep tanks and vehicles with treads, such as our tractor pulling guns and tanks, from penetrating the line. The Ninth Army had already penetrated the line that we were crossing. As we entered Germany, I could see my crew members riding beside me in our tractor snap into an electrifying alertness. They said nothing; there was no need for words. Napper, my gunner who was sitting on the opposite side of our tractor from me, clicked a bullet into the chamber of the carbine strung across his back and swung it forward. The crew realized that we were now riding through enemy territory.

My first observation upon entering Germany, beyond the "dragon teeth" on its border, was that the war had come to the German people with a sort of special spectacular violence that is not easy to describe. I found the destruction visited on these German towns and villages to be the worst site of unbelievable destruction I had seen up to this point. No destruction observed during our four days of travel from Utah Beach to the outskirts of Paris and then to Belgium compared with that levied on the western section of Germany. It was not long before our column reached a village called Richterich on the fringe of the Hurtgen Forest about thirty miles inside Germany. The weather

CHAPTER 4

was clear and cold on this morning, and the roads were wet, slippery, and in poor condition as a result of constant shelling. The first snow of the season had fallen in this part of Germany the previous night, but it melted quickly, accounting for the slippery roads.

As we reached our previously selected site, we pulled in and set up a command post, which directed our fire on distant targets and occasionally on fixed and approaching targets. This place was little more than a country crossroad, with the German version of a general store and three or four farmhouses. We parked astride a narrow dirt road that overlooked a rolling green valley. This gave us a good range of fire. A small dark forest of pine trees mounted to the hills beyond. None of us knew that this simple forest would become a major battleground in the very near future. We placed our guns along the fringes of the road on the tips of the forest and placed our tractor prime movers in several dugout encampments, which the retreating Germans had carved out of the hillside just a few days ago.

CHAPTER 5

In Battle in Europe

As described by Edward G. Miller in "A Dark and Bloody Ground," in late 1944 U.S. forces advanced into the heavily wooded Hurtgen Forest, which was located southwest of Aachen, Germany. The forest covered about thirty square miles. Without a clear-cut reason for attacking the Germans through the forest, U.S. commanders still ordered seven divisions into the Hurtgen Forest, only to be overrun by superior numbers of German infantry and artillery. Small U.S. units found themselves cut off by the rugged terrain and densely growing fir trees. Because of this landscape, they were unable to protect themselves by employing their tanks or artillery effectively. In addition, the troops were exposed to one of the coldest winters experienced in Germany in a century, without proper winter clothing.

In spite of these unfavorable conditions, U.S. troops were ordered to attack entrenched and camouflaged Germans in the woods. This was disastrous, resulting in many companies' suffering huge numbers of casualties, approximately fifty-five thousand killed or wounded.

For many years after the war the full extent of the disaster of the Hurtgen Forest campaign was not discussed or even well known outside army circles. Only in the last decade have military historians begun to look at the fighting that took place there.

Our engagement in the Hurtgen Forest campaign began on November 3, 1944—just several hours after our arrival in the firing zone. The purpose of the campaign was to occupy the western, industrial portion of Germany known as the Ruhr Pocket. This battle would constitute our participation in the Kohlscheid penetration; and as we arrived, it was already raging on the front line less than a mile away. It began from our position in Richterich, with the objective of reaching the Roer River. During the time of our location in Richterich, we functioned in support of the 30th Infantry Division. The forward element of this division was to attack the first German towns and cities leading into the Ruhr Pocket and the Hurtgen Forest for one week. By the time we arrived, the division's efforts had already exacted a heavy toll in both lives and wounded.

We received our first real baptism by fire during the savage offensive action against German bastions in the Jülich section of the Kohlscheid front on November 3. Accounts of the kind of fight we put up at such a bitterly contested town as Richterich became favorite topics of discussion among hard-bitten soldiers whose day-to-day lives were filled with the whiplash of the sudden terror of enemy mortar and artillery fire and the sickly penetrating odor of newly spilled blood. Since the beginning of our battalion's engagement there, more than three thousand rounds of our artillery had been fired. When we entered the Kohlscheid penetration scene, it was strangely reminiscent of a Hollywood movie set. Its surreal look included sleek black-and-white Holstein cattle, which the Germans had confiscated from throughout conquered Europe, grazing in the vast valley just below us and stopping at times to raise their heads and stare curiously at us. However, the firing of our first adjustment rounds sent these beasts stampeding down the valley, where they disappeared. Although they had grazed there quietly just minutes before, like rational beasts, they pocketed their pride and ran in search of safety. As we advanced our firing position at daybreak, bodies of German soldiers littered the landscape, a testament to our first night in combat on the western front.

At the same time, in the flatlands just beside us, I saw German women plowing, breaking the half-frozen ground for winter planting. They waded ankle deep in mud, their shoulders hunched against the uneven padding of the white oxen pulling the plows, as there was no fuel for mechanical plowing. Their hands were locked hard on the plow handles, with no hope of relief until they had completed the job of turning the hard soil. Farther down as we moved along to our next firing position, to my left, a young farm boy tended a flock of sheep in a pasture at the edge of a forest. I was certain that this was a firing position for German artillery just two days ago. An aged woman lingered disconsolately among the wreckage of a bombed-out farmhouse in the back of my gun position. It may have been her home at one time. Looking down, I noticed a lacelike green froth on the surface of a pool of stagnant water in a shell hole—adding even more to the surreal air of the surrounding scene.

Our attacks as we moved toward the Roer River were very difficult because of several natural barriers, as well as artificial barriers constructed by the Germans. The first was the Hurtgen Forest, which was difficult to maneuver. The forest posed special hazards, as it was thickly wooded and cut by steep defiles, firebreaks, and trails. Overall, the terrain of the Hurtgen Forest was ideally suited to the defense, with its dense primordial woods of tall fir trees, deep gorges, high ridges, and narrow trails. In addition, the Germans had built deep artillery-proof bunkers surrounded by fighting positions. They placed thousands of antipersonnel and tank mines throughout the floor of the forest. Systematically, they felled trees across the roads and wired, mined, and booby-trapped them, while registering and focusing their artillery, mortars, and machine guns on the roadblocks.

To the Roer River

The drive through the towns on the edge of the Hurtgen Forest in early November was supposed to be part of a limited offensive to reach the Roer River, but it turned out to be a major battle and the bloodiest yet to be fought on the western front. The German units had been retreating across Europe and settled here in these formidable defensive positions to make a final—and trying—effort to inflict heavy casualties on our forces. The canopy of trees on the fringe of the forest was so dense that the shadows created by the sun shining through their leaves left intriguing patterns on the seemingly flat forest floor, now blanketed by the powder of one of Germany's worst snowstorms in centuries.

Unfortunately, even though we were aware of the crystalline tree branches, which drooped under the weight of ice, I doubt that any of us could appreciate the beautiful wintry scene, as the cracking sounds of those branches kept all of us jumpy. After all, we were in our enemy's homeland now, and they knew every trail and walkway. It was not long until the high artillery shells exploded, sending thousands of lethal splinters downward and making movement across towns near the forest even more hazardous. Incoming enemy artillery shells struck twenty-five to thirty feet in the air, jolting ground troops with maximum killing capacity. We suffered our first casualty due to enemy action when a German 150-mm artillery shell exploded in one of our gun positions. Lt. James Wright died later that day of wounds suffered in the attack, which also wounded several other crew members, who were treated in our makeshift aid station for the firing batteries. Our guns fired 2,834 rounds from this position during the night and throughout the day. That evening, at approximately dusk, our battalion was ordered up for closer support of our infantry division and a tank battalion, which was under a counterattack by the German 1st and 5th Panzer Divisions. We fired all night and were able to help repel the attack. By sunrise, 3,284 shells had been fired. In the event of a German breakthrough in our line, alternative firing positions were prepared near Herzogenaurach. Later, a second group of alternate firing positions was established near North Brandenburg.

The next morning, while we were replenishing our ammunition supply, I noticed trucks passing my gun position at a slow pace. The truck drivers appeared to be driving slowly to protect their cargo. At first, I thought they were ammunition trucks returning from the front a few hundred yards ahead of us. The column was more than a mile long, and the trucks were evenly spaced. They continued passing by for such a long time that it seemed the convoy would never end. Then, as one truck came by, I thought I saw a wristwatch-clad arm swing out from under the tarpaulin covering one of the truck beds. I walked a few paces to the road and pulled the end of the tarpaulin up to find that the truck's cargo consisted of dead American soldiers just killed in the forest. The dead soldier with the wristwatch was laid flat on his back—a short lifetime etched on his young face—one that would see no more birthdays, anniversaries, or even the smile on a future grandchild's face. These killings were different from those occurring on the beaches on

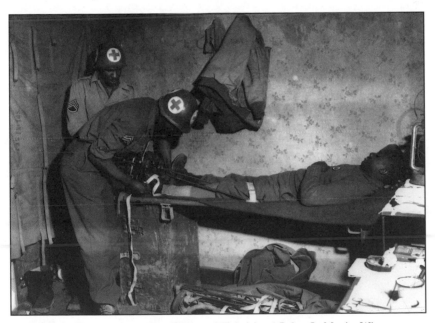

S.Sgt. W. B. Hoser, Houston, Texas (left), and Technician 4 Robert L. Martin, Wharton, Texas (center), put a splint on a soldier's leg at a field artillery battalion's medical aid station near Übach, Germany. The medics were attached to the Headquarters Battery of the battalion. Their patient, Pfc. Hayward M. Crawford, New Orleans, Louisiana, was a former track star at Xavier University in New Orleans.

D-day and in the fighting across France. In those cases, our solders died and were buried in friendly territory. The army had, and still has, a policy of not burying our dead solders in enemy territory, so they were being hauled out to receive proper burial on hallowed grounds. Ironically, the same trucks we met on the highway just two days ago that were being used to haul German prisoners were now hauling out our dead soldiers killed just a few miles inside the German border.

When the hearses brought in their daily cargo of dead soldiers from the front, colored burial details sought them out by the hundreds. These young American dead were then sprawled out in separate piles, their bloodstained, torn uniforms soaked black with silt from the gumbo muck so that they looked like heaps of abandoned rubble. It had been raining a thin, bitter drizzle that turned the burial fields into quagmires. I discovered later that the burial organization was the 611th Quartermaster Graves Registration Company and the ground the dead soldiers were lying on would become part of their cemetery. One of the trucks was loaded with colored soldiers, who had the job of classifying and burying the dead. At a distance I heard the white company captain tell the soldiers that their cemetery would grow. This type of work was unpleasant, but they were fortunate because they were not the victims. They were still alive and well. I could see that the soldiers getting off the truck were mesmerized and, in some cases, horrified by the piles of dead bodies lying before them. Some just could not take the first sight of the bodies of men, some still warm, killed in battle. Before we left our position to advance forward, one medic told me some twenty-one thousand had been buried. A few soldiers broke rank and rushed toward the nearest latrine to empty their stomachs. One medic sergeant commented, "Gruesome, ain't it? Sure is gruesome. I can't handle working here—I'm going to the grave-digging detail. Give me a shovel, I'm gonna dig graves." He grabbed a pointed shovel, stepped over several bodies, and walked through the mud, shaking his head as he walked along until he was in the open field of the cemetery. This all took place while we were in a small Dutch village not too far from the German frontier city of Aachen.

November gave way to December, and the drizzling rains turned to bitter cold and icy winds. The frozen soil was iron hard, requiring soldiers up to four hours to dig a single grave. But with December and that arctic cold, the number of casualties from the front declined rapidly. In November, the hearses brought in hundreds of casualties each day, but now the number trickled down to a few dozen daily. In spite of the frozen ground, the crew worked swiftly so the bodies would not be left unburied overnight.

CHAPTER 5

The German towns of Richterich, Übach, and Geilenkirchen were on the fringe of the Hurtgen Forest. Aachen, which held great symbolic importance to the German ideology, was a major city in the forest and was heavily defended by the German forces. Birthplace of Charlemagne, it invoked memories of the glories of the Holy Roman Empire and had captured Hitler's imagination. "The city," the führer ordered, "must be held at all costs." The garrison at Aachen fought stubbornly, surrendering on October 21 after two final weeks of hand-to-hand and house-to-house combat. The Germans put up heavy resistance, defending all of the towns in or on the fringe of the forest, and inflicted heavy casualties on our invading forces. During the time of our location at Richterich, we were attached to the 202nd Field Artillery Group and were in direct support of the 30th Infantry Division. From this position 6,118 rounds were fired.

On December 2, we cleared positions near Richterich and advanced to new ones approximately one mile southeast of Übach. We made several lateral advances in the Übach area, firing 1,575 rounds in direct infantry support. We remained in the vicinity of Übach until December 21, when an advance was started to new positions 1.8 miles south of Geilenkirchen. We occupied our new firing positions on December 21 at 7:20 A.M. and fired our first rounds at 7:30. We fired 400 rounds during the night from this position. Finally, we advanced a second time at daylight from our Geilenkirchen location. It seemed strange that immediately after we evacuated this position, the truck convoy parked about eight hundred yards behind us began loading dead soldiers. The soldier pallbearers were trained for this job and were very efficient. They stacked the dead soldiers like cords of wood. They had been trained to collect and bury the dead, just as I had been trained to kill and to try to keep from being killed.

As we moved on a few hundred yards forward, we finally could see the surprising impact of the forest shelling. It was clear that the exploding shells from both sides of the line had cut paths, almost like roads, through the tree canopy. These paths allowed shafts of sun to shine directly on the bloodstained snow. As we reached a clearing a few yards outside this thick canopy, we came upon three Sherman tanks on fire. Seemingly, they had been ambushed. Six tankers were lying on the ground partially covered with snow. Half a body was extending out of the top turret of one tank; three of the tankers were dead; the battle jacket of one was red with blood from multiple wounds; and another was already almost covered with snow and lying on the ground—although we could not discern immediately if he was dead or alive. The tank nearest my moving tractor was also on fire, and a tanker who had been trying to escape through his top turret but was too weak to make the final pullout had been shot. The unusual odor that emitted from the burning tanks had none of the chemical smell usually associated with burning fuel or machine components. I noted that it had to be the smell of burning human flesh. Despite the approaching heat from the flames, the tanker who had been shot during his escape attempt was still lying there with half of his body slumped on the turret, not responding to the approaching fire. I jumped off my tractor while it was still running and ran to the burning tank. I attempted to climb on top of the hot piece of steel, but it was extremely high and difficult to climb. I later discovered that the Sherman tanks were equipped with big airplane engines and were higher off the ground than the sleek, low German tiger tanks. As I climbed up on the tank, I realized that the tanker was still alive but only half conscious. He kept repeating in a low tone, "Where were you last night; where were you last night?" He was referring to our artillery. It was just sunrise, about 5:00 A.M., but it was clear that in his semiconscious state he was focused on a short time earlier—about the time of their attack by the Germans when he was first wounded. Since the burning tank was still under severe small-arms and mortar fire, I hastily pulled him from the turret to prevent his falling back into the tank. This permitted me to look through the turret, where I saw three tankers half consumed with flames and still buckled in their seats—apparently killed by some explosion before they even had a chance to escape. I noted that the tanker I was carrying to safety was probably the tank commander, but he bore no rank marking—this was customary to avoid being specifically targeted by the enemy. His green fatigues were soaked on the back with blood, which meant that he had been shot by the Germans while trying to crawl from his tank. I laid him down under a cypress tree on the edge of the forest, far enough away from what would have been his burning tomb to escape injury in the event his tank exploded. As I ran to rescue this soldier, the risk of the tank exploding while I was on or near it simply never crossed my mind. Obviously, my training as a field artilleryman had accomplished what it had set out to do—to keep me running on knowledge and adrenaline and, consequently, allowing no room for fear. The wounded soldier lost so much blood that he was in a twilight zone, suspended somewhere between life and death. There were so many dead here—the fields littered with bodies. I tried to answer his question by quickly explaining that last night we were in a killing field helping to turn back a German counterattack to prevent them from overrunning our lines; we literally had fired all night long.

CHAPTER 5

However, the tanker was drifting in and out of consciousness, so he probably did not hear me. Knowing that I had no choice at the moment but to move on, I put his knapsack under his head and hoped that the medics would find him before it was too late. If the medics did not see him soon, I knew the waiting trucks were not too far away, waiting to scoop up their dead cargo. I left and set my guns up for the morning engagement. Of course, I never knew the dying soldier's name. As many soldiers do when they think back on times such as these, I often wonder if he made it. At the time, though, when death and dying are continually surrounding you, the value of life appears to diminish. I found myself asking, why all the trouble? I suppose those thoughts are simply a defense mechanism, because you really do not want to end up dead. Even today, that question, "Where were you last night?" frequently appears in my dreams, but I can never get near enough to answer, and then the dream just fades out.

Our struggle advancing toward the Roer River continued for another two weeks. Finally, on December 5, we reached its west bank. After weeks of supporting the infantry fighting, the towns on the edge of the forest floor had taken on an appearance reminiscent of the ravaged "no-man's-land" of World War I. Wasted machines and shattered equipment were scattered throughout the forest towns, and the stench from bodies left in the open was almost unbearable. Unfortunately, the dead were destined to wait for our grave registration teams to move them from the forest, as so many wounded swamped the overtaxed evacuation. The German dead remained for even longer periods of time.

Aside from the stench of death, two months of supporting the bloody, close-quarters fighting in mud, snow, and cold added to the devastation of morale. In time, when the uncollected bodies were finally covered with the snow, parts of at least three U.S. divisions, pushed beyond all human limits, experienced breakdowns of both cohesion and discipline. The struggle to clear the fringe town of the Hurtgen Forest cost our armed forces approximately fifty-five thousand dead and wounded. (The figure on p. 67 shows American infantrymen who were engaged in this struggle.)

As early as December 1944, one of our corps commanders had reported to the supreme commander that his army group lacked seventeen thousand riflemen because of the high casualties caused by prolonged combat and constant exposure to the severe winter weather. Since November, we had been fighting in bitter winter weather, dealing with frostbite and trench foot, as challenging, and as dangerous, as battling the enemy. Although our supreme commander ordered the reclassification of as many support personnel as possible to provide relief to weary troops, we soon began to experience a shortfall that continued to grow. A call for troops to repel the latest German counterattack in the Ardennes-Alsace campaign only made the shortage more critical. Quite simply, even the U.S. selective service system could not close the increasing manpower gap.

As a result, Supreme Commander Eisenhower made a momentous decision. Previously, most African American soldiers in the European theater had been assigned to service units. I saw them during our four-day journey across France in isolated outposts along the lonely roads, all the way through Belgium. I saw long lines of African American hands resting on steering wheels as truck convoys thundered past our slow-moving column of guns. But now, Eisenhower was allowing these troops to volunteer for duty as combat unit infantrymen with the understanding that after the necessary training, they would be committed to front-line service. Eventually, twenty-two hundred were organized into fifty-three platoons and assigned to all-white rifle companies in the two U.S. Army groups. The shortage of combat soldiers temporarily had forced the army to discard its racist policy of segregating white and colored soldiers. The forces of necessity here most certainly played a role in spurring the civil rights movement in the United States twenty years later. Historical records illustrate the magnitude of the racist army policy: only eleven out of the seventy-seven African American army units in the European theater of operations were assigned to combat duties, even after the policy was implemented.

From the Roer to the Rhine

We pulled up to the west bank of the Roer River, immediately dug in, and set up to fire. We were long overdue for a breather—at least long enough to be resupplied and allow for replacements. We all simply needed a day off, both sides, on this Christmas Eve 1944. Our fight to the Roer had taken its toll on all of our units, both in lives and equipment. Late that evening we were moving back to the edge of the town when suddenly something hit our tractor prime mover number 1 with a powerful explosion. The crew had just dismounted and was positioning the gun to fire. The explosion from a German 88-mm gun shell happened right in front of the tractor. Our chief of the firing battery, Sergeant Cole, was standing nearby and was blown almost up into the seat of the tractor. He was unconscious but still standing, with his hand gripped on the tractor steering. I rushed to pull him into an area of protection, as the German battery of 88-mm guns had zeroed in

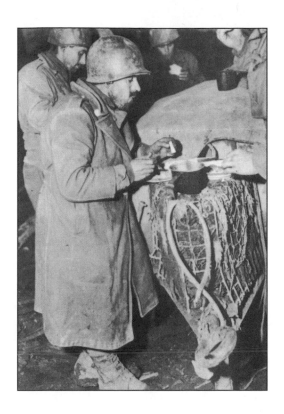

Tired, dirty, and hungry 30th Division infantrymen after fifteen days of siege at Hurtgen Forest.

on our position and surely other shells would follow. I caught him before he fell. There were no visible signs of injury on his face or arms, but he was bleeding from his mouth and eyes. Our battalion medic came and removed Sergeant Cole, who died shortly thereafter from internal injuries caused by the blast. Three other cannoneers were also wounded and were taken away by the medics. I did not see them anymore, so I am not sure if they made it, if their wounds were life threatening, or even if they were taken out of the line and sent home. The next three rounds fired by the German battery went over our position. This gave us time to set up to fire and the opportunity to locate the position of the German battery. We destroyed it in two rounds of fire. The Germans had other 88-mm gun batteries in the line, but they were too well hidden to locate. Three days and nights of deadly fighting ensued. Along with our infantry, we inflicted heavy losses on the German tanks and troops while they continued to inflict losses on us.

The morning after Sergeant Cole's death I was promoted to his position and awarded a certificate of merit for my chief of section activities since the beginning of the Roer River campaign. I went from chief of section of Battery B to being responsible for the firing by all four guns in the battery, or chief of the firing battery. Our primary objective was to clear resistance in the area, make preparations for crossing the Roer River, and make the twenty-five-mile run to the west bank of the Rhine River. This by far was the greatest natural obstacle before us and was the symbolic frontier of the German homeland.

Suddenly we heard, then clearly saw, the planes. It was not long before I began to believe that the Germans were sending out their entire air force. In fact, I had never seen so many German planes before, and I was not exactly sure what it was all about. Thankfully, the snow and ice from the deep freeze were thawing. On Christmas morning 1944, about one thousand German Messerschmitt (ME) 109s and Focke-Wulf 190s took off from snow-covered fields all over Germany. Grouped in four large wings and observing absolute radio silence, they flew westward, guided by a single Junker 88 bomber. As they approached the front, the Junker turned back and the wings were directed to their targets by colored smoke, searchlights, and Christmas trees. At 8:05 A.M., a small Taylor artillery-spotting aircraft, which carried no weapons, was flying over the Allied front when it spotted part of the aerial armadas. The pilot radioed back a frantic message, "The howitzers just passed a formation of at least two hundred Messerschmitts flying low on course three-two-zero." It was the first indication to Allied high command that Hitler had surprised them again. German intelligence had worked out the location of every Allied air base, and now every pilot was given a large-scale map on which these bases were clearly marked, together with return courses, landmarks, and detailed routing instructions. They were going to take out every one of those bases. In the end, American pilots who managed to become airborne shot down thirty-six German planes. By 10:30 Christmas morning, it was all over—nearly one hundred German planes had been put out of action, but the Germans had succeeded in wrecking three hundred Allied planes and knocking out twenty-seven Allied bases. Goering's Big Blue, as the operation was code-named, was an astonishing success, brilliantly worked out, and superbly executed, according to American high command.

They flew over our position, but our guns were well camouflaged, so I was not sure if they saw us. Next, I heard a roaring sound above that seemed to disappear as quickly as it appeared. I soon surmised that it was the first jet plane I had ever seen or heard. I found out later that it was the new ME 262—a German jet and the first jet fighter-bomber in existence. Hitler had issued a new generation of weapons to terrorize his enemies into coming to terms with his conditions. Ten minutes later, I heard the sound of two different motors and looked up. What I saw was a real dogfight between an American P-47 fighter-bomber and a German ME 109 fighter.

The planes were evenly matched, and the fight ensued for several minutes. Finally, I saw smoke trailing the German plane. As the plane started to dive, a parachute popped into the air. I waited for its descent and anticipated that I would take the German pilot prisoner. The descent took so long that I realized the dogfight took place at a higher altitude than I had estimated. When I looked up again, I saw the pilot free-falling because the parachute never fully opened. Usually when this happens, the pilot screams before hitting the ground, but this one hit the ground and bounced back into the air without making a sound. I rushed over, took his parachute off, and discovered that his ripcord had a knot in it, making it impossible to open the parachute. The packaging of the parachute appeared to be an act of sabotage. A high percentage of factory workers in Germany during the war were not native Germans but foreigners, allowing the possibility of sabotage. Upon his fall, the pilot hit the ground on his back and left the bulk of the parachute to serve as a buffer against any external mutilation of his body. Killed instantly, his body left an imprint in the deep snow, bouncing approximately two feet up before settling. Amazingly, despite all of this movement, his face remained visibly unharmed, and his pilot's cap had shielded him from any external head injuries. I thought I saw steam coming from his mouth as if he were attempting to breathe, but I soon realized that it was steam generated by the heat of his still-warm body in the snow. What caught my attention when I looked closely at him was that he appeared somehow different from the German soldiers we encountered daily in the field. I suppose the reason was that he was dressed in clean clothes and had a clean, youthful face, in contrast to the typical German foot soldier, who was generally older and appeared stressed and unkempt.

Apparently the P-47 base was nearby, because in about an hour the pilot came back to the scene. He looked at the dead German pilot and said his real regret was that he had a son in Ohio about the same age. Other than some air activity, there was a lull in the fighting on both sides. It was the quietest day we had experienced since the Roer River campaign had begun. The world seemed so bright with the sun shining on the white snow, and I even thought I had heard singing just after sunset coming from over the snow. Was it just a dream? That would have been a rarity since we slept with our clothes on in a type of sleeping bag that unzipped quickly in case of an attack. If we kept a firing position for two days or more, we dug a hole about five feet deep and six to seven feet wide and covered it with a tarpaulin and a camouflaged net to keep the snow out—this was home for a few days.

We dug a trench two by two feet wide and eight feet long for waste disposal. Our helmets became our washbasins, and our only food source was K rations. Eleven men could enter the dugout at one time if it were fully occupied. Two cannoneers were always out standing guard for the crew, preventing surprise attacks. These dugouts had been our homes since our first night here on the western front.

Again I heard singing, but it was barely audible. Perhaps I am dreaming, I thought. But a few Germans were entertaining themselves by singing a song I had read about called "Lili Marlene." I think they must have wanted us to hear their singing.

The lyrics of "Lili Marlene" were written by Hans Leip in 1915 and translated into English by Tommie Connor in 1944. The German Afrika Korps was often shown on newsreels singing and marching to the rhythm of this song.

> Underneath the lantern, by the barrack gate
> Darling, I remember the way you used to wait.
> T'was there that you whispered tenderly
> That you loved me, you'd always be
> My Lili of the Lamplight, my own Lili Marlene.
> Time would come for roll call, time for us to part.
> Darling I'd caress you and press you to my heart,
> And there 'neath that far-off lantern light,
> I'd hold you tight, we'd kiss good night,
> My Lili of the Lamplight, My own Lili Marlene.

Then again I thought, as the singing continued, it could just as easily be coming from British troops, as they were only a short distance from us down our line. In fact, just before I left England, I saw a column of British soldiers marching and singing by keeping the rhythm of "Lili Marlene." Lying back, I almost let myself completely relax—I experienced some inner peace for a short while. As I took in the scene of the deep snow around us, I was suddenly reminded that Christmas had arrived—although neither side celebrated. Without the peaceful sound of this music, I would have forgotten all about the holiday. During reflective times, words such as these from Shakespeare's *Love's Labour's Lost* would run through my head: "At Christmas I no more desire a rose than wish a snow in May's newfangled mirth; but like of each

Soldiers of the 777th Field Artillery Battalion near Übach, Germany, sit in a dugout near their guns waiting for firing orders. The medic on duty with them, shown with a red cross on his helmet, is Pvt. Veerland Thompson, Newport, Virginia. The soldiers are left to right: Pvt. Lester Rutland, Sylvester, Georgia; Cpl. Robert Jones, Longbranch, Texas; Pfc. Lafayette Owens, Anniston, Alabama; Cpl. Ellis W. McNeal, Eufaula, Oklahoma; Pfc. James P. Laney, Beaumont, Texas; Pfc. Tommy L. Dickerson, Texarkana, Texas; and Pvt. Lloyd E. Arrington, Chicago, Illinois.

thing that in season grows." My mind invented its own way to provide me with brief escapes from my current surroundings.

We had been alerted that the Germans were trying to penetrate our lines by dropping agent paratroopers behind our lines. Early one morning, I went around alerting our guards to be especially vigilant because these suspected German agents were dressed in U.S. uniforms and pretending to be American. For our defense, we had a password that everyone was required to know. In addition, we had been told that words containing the letter *r* were difficult for Germans to pronounce. On my way back to our gun position I saw a plane appear just above the tree line directly in front of me. At first I thought it was a U.S. P-51 fighter as it headed straight toward me at a blinding speed. When it got closer, I saw an iron cross on the engine cover and recognized it as a German Messerschmitt 109. I could have fired at him in his cockpit with my carbine, but everything happened so rapidly. For some strange reason, at that moment, I did not want to kill him, which

I could have at that close range, even at his high speed. My first instinct was to take cover behind any solid object nearby, which happened to be a large cypress tree about ten paces to my right, but he was too close and his fire was directed between myself and the tree as if he anticipated my protective move. I froze in my tracks without even falling to the ground. I could see the pilot's face by now. He was right on me—almost close enough to strike me with the wing of his plane. At the same time I saw flashes from the leading edge of his wing and to my right between myself and the cypress tree and a bullet trail in the snow left from the firing of his plane's wing guns. Then he ceased firing, headed up, and passed over me. I stopped and sat on a wood stump covered with snow a few paces to my left. I had to get myself together. I kept wondering why he did not kill me. I am sure he saw me walking across the open field and had dived, heading straight toward me, to kill me but then changed his mind. Just two hours earlier I had witnessed one of his pilots killed but under different circumstances. Then my instinctive feelings surfaced, and I thought that in spite of this brutal, bloody war, good could emerge, even in the heart of the enemy. Perhaps he spared my life because it was Christmas. Christmas 1944 carries a special meaning to me even after all these years. Maybe all of us just wanted to stop killing each other for a while. He came so close to me that the fumes from the fuel of his plane permeated the air and my clothes long after he pulled up and passed over me. The battle for the Roer River raged on.

The battle of the Roer River was really a battle for control of the dams on the river. The battles turned out to be about as costly in American lives as the campaign for the towns on the fringe of the Hurtgen Forest. The Roer River was dammed in seven places; the largest was the Schwammenauel, which was 180 feet high. German engineers could open the dams at any time, which made the river totally impassable. Twenty-five miles east of the Roer was the Rhine, one of the largest and fastest flowing in Europe. Engineers using models of the Roer and its surrounding area tried to predict what would happen to the Roer if the Germans flooded the river and how our attack forces would cope. Our commanders were confident that all obstacles could be overcome. In addition to the fixed defenses, the Germans had improvised several tactics to prevent our forces from crossing the Roer. Speedboats were packed with one hundred pounds of explosives and aimed at bridges and pontoons constructed by our engineers. The crew would jump off at the last moment as the boat raced in to its target. The German soldiers defending the river were under orders never to give ground. If forced to withdraw, they were to leave nothing intact for the enemy to use. Every bridge and every

Crossing the Roer River. Source: Pictoral Records Center for Military History, Washington, D.C., 340, 1951.

vehicle that could not be taken away was to be destroyed. The Germans made the price of invading Germany as difficult and as costly as possible.

On February 10, 1945, the Roer dams finally were seized. Although the Germans had not blown them up as we feared, they had destroyed the discharge valves. Instead of the anticipated massive flood, a steady flow of water gradually inundated the Roer valley. The flooding of the Roer delayed our attack until February 23, when we participated in the artillery preparation that furnished a division to support the attack of the XIII Corps. Two thousand rounds were expended in this operation. In the early morning of February 23, we folded our guns and crossed the still-flooded Roer River, surprising the Germans. By the end of the day, approximately twenty-eight battalions had crossed the Roer and firmly established a bridgehead.

On March 1, we occupied a position in the vicinity of Haar, Germany. We made a night march from Haar to Heidhausen without incident. After a day in rendezvous, we moved out to occupy positions in the vicinity of Weier. From this position, we had a night of the heaviest firing in our history. Our battalions fired more than thirteen hundred rounds in a single night. From here, in the presence of corps commanders and the corps artillery commander, my gun, number 3, Battery B, fired the first rounds of artillery for the XVI Corps across the Rhine into Mehrum, Germany. Positions were reconnoitered, prepared, and occupied on March 6, near Altfeld. From this position we fired directly on barges, vehicles, and troop-assembly points in the pocket south of Wesel and west of the Rhine River. We sank several barges and destroyed German vehicles. In addition, our air observation posts had several field days firing on the artillery batteries that were trying to protect the crossing of the Germans to the east bank of the Rhine River. These batteries were destroyed or silenced.

On March 10 we reconnoitered for and prepared positions in the vicinity of Rheinkamp under corps orders. From these positions, my battalion assisted in the artillery preparation for the crossing of the Rhine River by the XVI Corps, which was to effect the initial crossing for the Ninth Army. This position was occupied on March 12. The mission of the battalion was to support and reinforce the firing of the 79th Artillery Division.

As our forces consolidated after crossing the Roer and prepared for the main thrust to the Rhine, the movement of different forces created a squeeze on the Rhine. Aachen, the first German city captured, and its relation to the West Wall (the Siegfried line) and our path across the Hurtgen Forest are illustrated on the map on p. 75. Items to note are the Roer River, the Schwammenauel Dam, and the twenty-five-mile distance between the Roer River and the Rhine. Essen, Duisberg, and Düsseldorf are some German cities our forces captured during the bloodiest battles of the war, which took place in the Roer valley and the Rhine River campaigns.

Even before our three Allied army groups advanced up to the Rhine, they had begun to plan for the final crossing. Field Marshal Montgomery's 21st Group had planned an amphibian crossing, code-named Operation Plunder. For the attack, naval land craft had been transported to the front. Thousands of tons of supplies also had been stockpiled, with three full-strength armies and five thousand artillery pieces all poised for the Rhine crossing. Our commanders intended to seize a substantial bridgehead over the Rhine and then to maintain a monumental strike deep into Germany. Operation Plunder would be reinforced by Operation Varsity. A powerful landing by the U.S. 7th Airborne Division and the British 6th Airborne Division with three thousand aircraft and gliders would be dropped east of the Rhine to enlarge the bridgehead. Operations Plunder and Varsity were scheduled to begin on March 24.

The article below was published on March 4, 1945, in the U.S. Army newspaper, *Stars and Stripes,* and was broadcast over Luxembourg radio to

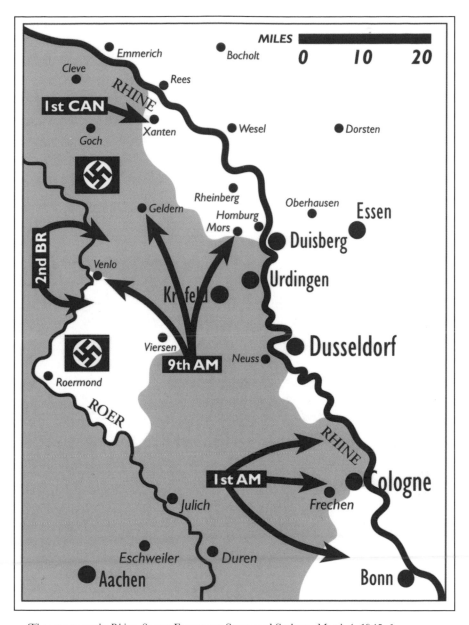

The squeeze on the Rhine. Source: European Stars and Stripes, *March 4, 1945, 1.*

the German civilians about the danger of lost lives during the impending Rhine River crossing.

> "Don't Flee Homes Ike Tells Germans." General Eisenhower yesterday told German civilians west of the Rhine to stay where they are for every attempt to evacuate means immediate danger of death from allied artillery and air bombardment. Instructions were broadcast over the Luxembourg radio, Reuter reported. Declaring that there is no security east of the Rhine, Ike told the Germans all roads to the Rhine and its crossing will be overcrowded with fleeing German troops and will be kept under artillery and air bombardment. He urged the civilians to avoid a "senseless bloodbath."

Crossing the Rhine

After reaching the Rhine River, we adjusted and calculated our field of fire and dug in for a few days to catch up with supplies and much-needed ammunition. We spent a few days cleaning our guns, prepared fuses for our shells, and made preparations for the push across the Rhine, which we knew was scheduled. It was January and blusteringly cold, but the sun was shining brightly. A knoll near my guns was covered with green grass, so I lay down. Before falling asleep, I heard soldiers saying, "You had better take care of your chief." I awakened five hours later just after dusk, and as I looked up, I was surprised to see Orion, Sirius, and Arcturus still shining as bright and young as when the shepherd first saw them in the plains of Shinar. I recall having had a terrible nightmare while asleep. I dreamed that a German 88-mm shell exploded in my gun pit and killed my crew. I thought I was dead but was still trying to say something before the pallbearers came and picked us up. I kept mumbling as I tried to recall the statement Juliet made about Romeo:

> *When he shall die*
> *Take him and cut him out in little stars*
> *and he will make the face of heaven so fine*
> *That all the world will be in love with the night*
> *and pay no worship to the garish sun.*

Two crew members were standing over me when I finally woke from the horrible nightmare. They saw me struggling but did not know I was trying to get out of this terrible dream. I did not sleep anymore that night.

Crew digging in as preparation for firing mission across the Rhine River. Notice that one crew member carries a carbine in case of a small-arms attack.

The next morning the 777th Field Artillery Battalion fell into formation to hear messages read by representatives of Field Marshal Bernard Montgomery; our XVI Corps commander; and Battery A commander, Capt. Richard Worth, a white man from San Benito, Texas. As we assembled, I noticed my cannoneers were standing and listening in attentive silence, their squared shoulders standing out in sharp silhouette against a backdrop of scrub pine trees and barbed-wire entanglements implanted by the Germans as defensive mechanisms. Field Marshal Montgomery's personal message was read aloud to us first. In his message there was indeed the promise of "good hunting." The first faint warning of approaching twilight crept across the German lowlands with a sinister beauty. Captain Worth stood stiff at attention before delivering his message, holding a printed sheet of paper rigidly in one hand. He read from the printed page in a clear, firm voice, as reported by Theodore Stanford in the *Pittsburgh Courier* on April 15, 1945:

It is the seventh hour before the beginning of the struggle to cross the
Rhine River. In the west the enemy has lost the Rhineland and with
it the flower of at least four armies. We know something of the battles

Placing fuses in shells in preparation for firing. Pvt. Agelbert C. Cobb, Chicago, Illinois, Ninth Army Artilleryman of the 777th Field Artillery Battalion, removes safety pin from fuse of 4.5-inch shell.

for the Rhineland. Our battalion was the first colored combat troop outfit to fight on German soil. We earned that distinction the day we set up our batteries on a field's edge beyond the ruined German town of Richterich.

The Russian armies are within thirty-five miles of Berlin. We as artillerymen have more than a few things in common with our Russian allies. They too are strangers in a hostile country, fighting to bring peace and freedom to the European soil. We are representative of all those colored combat troops in Europe who have fought so vigorously and with such skill that the fleeing Germans bitterly referred to them as the black Russians.

The enemy has in fact been driven into a corner and he cannot escape. It is known that the German soldiers hold a profound respect for the weapons handled by our men. We as artillerymen are proud of our record of being able to fire three rounds of ammunition into the air before the projectile of the first round has hit its target. Our record for rapid occupation is no less distinguished. We have been known to leave the highway and enter a field, select gun positions, set up our field pieces and to fire the first shell against the enemy, all in the breath-taking space of fifteen minutes.

The complete and decisive defeat of the Germans is certain. In the days of his glory Hitler once remarked that the Negro was little better than a beast. Yet our battalion has been publicly congratulated for having the lowest rate of courts-martial and venereal diseases of any military outfit in the European Theatre of Operation. We also hold the honor of being first in military bearing and personal appearance. Our speed and accuracy of firing [are] uncontested—the best in the European Theatre of Operation. Ordnance inspectors said we have the best artillery pieces in the European Theatre of Operation. We also played a conspicuous role in the task of setting the taste of defeat on the tongues of the German supermen. Over the Rhine then let us go.

The captain's voice died out, and for a moment there was only the heavy silence and the last agony of sunset along the western heavens. Against the evening sky huge cones of black smoke coiled upward from bombed German towns and drifted slowly westward across the Rhine. It was 7:05 P.M. The captain wheeled sharply, saluted, and dismissed the battalion.

On March 23, full details of Operation Flash Point, an assault on the Rhine, were received. Everyone began running through the cypress trees and in the fields to their tanks and tractors on their way to engage in the assault. The stage was set, the players in place, the script in hand, and the mighty assault on the Rhine began. Data sheets were prepared for the firing that started at 1:00 A.M. on March 24, 1945. Battery B's gun number 3 was called for a fire mission. My crew quickly loaded and fired. This round was followed by a thunderous roar from five thousand guns of the XVI Corps firing simultaneously at targets across the Rhine. The fire was deafening, and the earth shook. The five thousand muzzle blasts exploding all at once made the earth appear to be on fire and gave the impression that hell itself had come to us.

The firing preparations lasted until 3:00 A.M., and supporting fire was delivered all through the rest of the morning. During the preparation for Operation Flash Point, our battalion exceeded the twenty-thousand-extended-round mark since entering the Rhineland campaign. At 3:00 A.M. we began our final preparations to cross the Rhine. I watched the sun rays start breaking the crescent of the eastern horizon as we approached the spot where the army engineers had built a pontoon bridge across the Rhine. As our slow-moving column approached the river, I noticed stray wisps of the early-morning fog hanging above the glassy surface of the river.

Newly constructed treadway pontoon bridge over the Rhine River. Source: Pictoral Records Center of Military History, Washington, D.C., 1951, 357.

We edged our way forward through the predawn light and heard the first German planes of the night. We scanned the skies and could not see the planes, but the drone of the motors was heavy and menacing. Our own antiaircraft guns sent up tracers that drove them off. The big artillery guns to our rear fired projectiles high above us as we moved closer to crossing the Rhine. Above the Rhine, a barrage of balloons soared like block sausages. The balloons gave some protection against low-flying aircraft that were attempting to attack our column while we were crossing. When the balloons were up in position, the enemy would not fly low over the river for fear of running into the cables holding the balloons in place.

We continued to roll down toward the bridge to begin our trip across. As we moved slowly forward, the pontoon bridge swayed from the weight of our tractors and guns. Some of our crew members expressed appreciation for the African American chemical engineers who laid down a smoke screen to conceal our exact position on the bridge as we crossed. We were helpless targets to both enemy aircraft and artillery fire during our amphibian crossing. It took four hours on the morning of March 25 for our entire battalion to cross the river. We ended up on a beachhead on the east side of the Rhine at daybreak. German resistance was scattered as we crossed the river. We occupied a position in the vicinity of Verden with our command post at the German town of Catherwickerham. As we rolled off the bridge, our battalion rushed forward onto the soil of inner Germany, marking the first time since the days of Napoleon that an invading army had stormed across the Rhine. Immediately after establishing a beachhead, we set up our position for firing, all in the predawn hours. Then the tanks, hundreds of them like sinister monsters searching for their prey, began to rumble forward, snapping off fir trees like matchsticks, destroying telephone lines, and turning German front-line positions into a churned-up lunar landscape. They anxiously took their turn to cross the pontoon bridge behind us.

Unfortunately, no one knew the level of resistance we would encounter as we attempted to establish this beachhead. A German garrison was once stationed a few miles from Verden, but our reconnaissance and intelligence did not show any German military training facilities in the area. Our planes had dropped leaflets to homeowners in the landing zone asking them to leave the area before it turned into a war zone. The supreme commander warned the civilians to stay put during our crossing of the Rhine or leave the area so as not to get caught in the crossfire, but they did not take the warning seriously. What we saw at sunrise was a horror scene of total devastation.

We discovered that there was a tunnel under the Rhine. German civilians mistook the sounds of the first rounds being fired from the west shore of the river as a signal to rush out and head to the tunnel for protection. They were ultimately caught in our artillery barrage and ended up in a pile of approximately four hundred dead corpses about four feet high. The dead were predominantly women and children, most dressed in sleeping clothes. On top of the pile was a blonde, teenage girl, about fifteen or sixteen, lying on her back. She had one shoe on—the other one was at the side of the stack of dead bodies on the ground. She looked as if she were asleep. I had seen thousands of dead people in towns near the forest and during the Ruhr campaign—but nothing like this. These people had actually suffered severe internal injuries from the concussion of our shells but had no visible signs of injury.

Another young woman was lying near a pile of bodies, next to a tall SS trooper. He was the only soldier among all the dead. They both lay near the rear of a roofless cottage a few yards to the right of another pile of bodies. She had fallen face down at the entrance of a small cellar under the cottage. They both were apparently heading for the cellar. From the markings on the ground made by the heels of the soldier's combat boots, he was not killed instantly but had struggled to get up. I think he must have bled to death. The young woman's starched black blouse and gray skirt were scarcely soiled. She wore an old-fashioned gold wedding band on her left-hand ring finger. Her slightly graying hair was neatly arranged and coiled in a bun at the nape of her neck. Both of her legs had been blown away at the knees. She looked awfully cramped and uncomfortable lying on the cold ground near a blood-colored rosebush. I think it was because she looked so prim and yet so pitiful that Napper, my gunner, reached out and turned her over with the butt of the carbine strapped across his shoulder. I will never be able to erase from my memory the death mask of her face. Her pointed nose was flattened against the damp earth. It had not rained recently, but the clouds were low and heavy fog added moisture to the soil. A smudge of dirt and a half-moist rose leaf clung to her right cheek. We all wondered if the young German soldier wearing the SS uniform lying next to her was her son.

I went over to my tractor prime mover, sat down on the bumper, and put my hands over my face. I am sure I was crying. In spite of the fact that I had become a killer, I was saddened to no end by this scene. While sitting there I noticed a hand was touching me and resting on my left shoulder. I looked to my left; I saw the hand was that of a white female. My natural instinct was to grab the carbine slung across my shoulder and whirl around to face the intruder. The hand was that of a Swiss Red Cross nurse. She was very gently saying something to me, but it was in German, so I did not understand her. I heard the word *bitte,* and I knew that meant "please." I turned and said "thank you" in German and walked away, as it was against army regulations to fraternize with the enemy in any form. Switzerland was a neutral country during World War II and was not considered our enemy, but on that morning of March 24, 1945, among all the dead surrounding me, any blonde female speaking German got my attention as being German—separating friend from foe was difficult at that moment. It was time to set up firing positions. I felt that I would never be the same person again because of the evils of war.

Before this tragedy, German soldiers were the enemy. In my mind, they were faceless. This feeling changed as I saw people walking among our gun positions in grief, trying to retrieve dead loved ones. Most of the searchers were silent, but some broke down in grief as a relative or friend was identified in the same way my mother, grandmother, or sister would. Humans react in about the same way, whether friend or foe, to occasions of great happiness, severe pain, or extreme sorrow. By midmorning, all of the corpses had been claimed and taken away. Most were moved by horse-drawn carriages. Many

CHAPTER 5

of the dead children were carried away in the arms of parents, loved ones, or friends. The sight of parents hugging the corpses of their dead children was indeed sad and heartbreaking.

In the past month, I had faced high-risk and near-death situations long enough to know some of us would remain behind in the grass, in a cypress tree forest, at the edge of a fast-flowing river, or on the corner of one of the bombed streets in some demolished village or city. The sun was now rising fast on the eastern horizon. The thick morning clouds were disassembling the sun's rays into individual shafts of light. The morning fog was gone. The sky was now blue. It was a beautiful day, but the face of the war had forever changed for me.

Through the Ruhr Pocket

As we expanded from our bridgehead in the vicinity of Verden, the rapid retreat of the Germans slowed as their resistance grew. As the battle raged farther into the Ruhr Pocket, the defenders became more determined. Before leaving the bridgehead, an advance party was sent to survey the area around Dinslaken to find a place to set up an observation post. We also needed an adequate location for our guns in the vicinity of our selected targets to provide direct support for our advancing infantry attack forces. Because of the flexibility and accuracy of our guns, we were leaving this bridgehead almost in concert with our infantry. Things were fluid and moving fast. At 8:00 A.M. on March 24, our advance party of three soldiers and I left Verden and headed for Dinslaken, about twenty miles north. Since our infantry was clearing resistance pockets as we advanced, the trip took about two hours by jeep.

Upon entering the outskirts of Dinslaken, I saw a large two-story house with an apple orchard located on the corner of two intersecting streets. With the support of an infantry platoon, we worked our way over to the house. We could get a view of enemy defensive fortifications for miles, as well as a view of troop movements, which made the house ideal for an observation post. The orchard was suitable for the location of our guns. Upon approaching the house, I stopped while our advancing infantry units kept moving. As we neared the house, I noticed it had two double glass doors at the front entrance and a wooden door on the west side. By peeking through the front doors, I could see stairs leading to the second floor, so we decided to approach through the front entry. Extreme caution had to be exercised, as a house this size could be the headquarters for German army units or could be used as an enemy hideout. We had just thirty minutes remaining to secure our position, as the battalion with our column of guns was scheduled to arrive at 10:30 A.M.

I walked in first, followed by three soldiers in support position with their carbines drawn. After a quick search, I found the downstairs vacant. I quickly, but cautiously, started upstairs. I walked on the balls of my feet to maintain silence on the oak stairs. Halfway up the stairs I heard talking and saw a pair of shoes worn by someone at the top of the stairs. They looked like men's shoes, but then I remembered they also looked like the shoes I had observed the women wearing as they plowed in the fields.

I looked up and saw a middle-aged woman standing at the top of the stairs. Her hands were raised and she was hysterically yelling "*Nicht schiessen, nicht schiessen, bitte nicht schiessen*" (Don't shoot, don't shoot, please don't shoot). I knew she was from a working family by the clothes she wore. I responded to her in the broken German I knew. "*Nicht Schiessen, nicht Schiessen, Frau—nicht Schiessen*" (No shooting, no shooting, lady, no shooting). By this time, three other individuals appeared at the top of the stairs and stood beside her. I alerted my assistants to be prepared in case an armed soldier appeared so that he would not get a drop on us.

As we advanced to the top of the stairs, the four retreated a few steps backward into a small kitchen area. I discovered that they were eating breakfast when we entered their home: a boiled egg, a slice of brown bread, a piece of meat, and coffee being served family style. The middle-aged woman nervously took a boiled egg from the table and offered it to me. I thanked her but refused. She appeared to have calmed down somewhat and tried to smile. In addition to the middle-aged woman, the group consisted of a young woman in her midthirties, a teenage girl, and an older man. I kept a watchful eye on them while my assistants searched the upstairs for armed soldiers.

During the search I had one of my assistants, who spoke German, explain to them that we would need their home for a few days as a headquarters, after which they could return. They took turns putting a few clothes in a gray handbag and finished eating the breakfast they had left on the table. I am not sure if the old man lived there or was just having breakfast, as he made no preparation to leave. He just stood at the window, gazing out over a large meadow. Perhaps he had once been a soldier but was now too old, so he was just waiting for the war to end with the women and children.

When the middle-aged woman first saw me, the enemy, with my weapon drawn and standing halfway up her stairs, she was frightened and I could see the panic in her eyes. I think it was from seeing the enemy in her house; and in the Ruhr area of Germany, many had never seen an African American man other than in films, books, and newspapers. The younger woman seemed too calm. She never seemed excited or afraid, which made me suspicious. The young girl was a little frightened, but I think she was more concerned about whether or not we would harm them. I think at first she was not sure if I was an African man or an American. She may have seen the American soldiers running while fighting in the streets, and they were all white, so I think she was confused. The old man seemed a little frightened, but mostly just apprehensive. I told them, through my interpreter, that they would have to leave and could live in a basement across the street for a few days. Then they could come back home. There was a big battle raging, and the basement would protect them. We were going to set our big guns up in their orchard, and we expected shelling from their soldiers. We had about ten minutes left before the arrival of our soldiers and guns, so I asked them to be out in five minutes and assured them we would do our best not to destroy their property.

Still, I remained vigilant while watching the young woman, suspicious that she might be a special agent. I had read in the *Stars and Stripes* about a soldier killed in the presence of a young German woman in Aachen. A few minutes before I walked out, the young woman asked me my name, *"Wie heissen Du?"* I was shocked and thought she was talking to someone else until I noticed she was looking at me. I told her, "Emiel Owens." The name got her attention, as she remembered Jessie Owens, plus Emil is a German name. She then walked up to me, rubbed her two fingers across my face and asked, *"Warum Du schwarz sind?"* (Why are you black?) *"Ist es die Sonne?"* (Is it the sun?) I told her the Negro race had many colors; it is not the sun, but race. She wanted a longer conversation, and so did I. I wanted to learn more about her. I had discovered that you cannot paint all Germans with one brush. I told her my time was up and for her to *"Gehen Sie schnell"* (leave quickly).

By this time, my guns were on the street, ready to be placed. We placed them among the fruit trees in her orchard, fired adjusting rounds, and were ready for our night firing. Our infantry was encountering stiff resistance in the center of the town and needed us. I saw the young woman again for the last time just before sunset that day, standing alone at the entrance of the cellar across the street from her home that we were occupying. The setting sun was in her face as she stood gazing toward our gun positions in her orchard. She had changed clothes to a pale blue outfit almost matching her steel blue eyes, but the relaxed composure she exhibited this morning seemed not to change.

This encounter stayed with me for a long time. As I first faced her, while going up the stairs that morning, I could see fear on her face but no panic. Foreign troops with black faces and drawn carbines occupying her home was a frightful experience for her, but she stayed calm as she became aware that we would not harm her. I later started thinking about my experience as a high school student with German American farmers at home. We were usually hired by them to pull corn during the peak corn-harvesting season. What I remembered most was that they ate four times a day, and someone would bring hot food to the field. They would lay a cloth on the ground, and everyone, including the hired hands, would sit to eat the food, which was served family style. This created a lasting impression, especially for youngsters who were struggling to get two meals daily at home.

We remained embroiled in battle for two days. Before we made our second advance in the Ruhr Pocket position, we were successfully occupied at Dinslaken. The position at Dinslaken was rather unusual for the size of our artillery because our battalion had the mission of covering a twelve-hundred-mil sector. All twelve of our guns were laid on a different centerline so that they could be massed on a five-hundred-mil sector in the center. Later, due to the risk of a counterattack by the Germans, all batteries were shifted to the left portion of the sector. At the close of the period, our battalion advanced to a position near Thurohdenwind with an azimuth of fire due east. During this cycle, 8,987 rounds were expended, the highest total for a month since we entered combat. This brought the total expended to date to 30,000 rounds. As we advanced farther into the interior of the Ruhr Pocket, we engaged in nearly three weeks of difficult and frustrating action. Although some cities surrendered at once, others made fanatical last stands in bombed-out streets and among the rubble in the middle of Germany's heartland.

Our advances became more frequent but for shorter distances. This gave us the opportunity to get a panoramic view of a once-proud nation that was now a conquered shell. During our advances, I observed untended fields pockmarked with foxholes and slit trenches covering the countryside. For the first time I saw that entire towns were devastated. The engine of my tractor roared hollowly through the streets of deserted villages, where not even the presence of migrating birds interrupted the lifelessness of the gutted buildings, the gaping shell holes, and the heaps of rubble. The silence in the towns was worse than the noise our shells made. Instinctively, we expected to hear the noises people make while going about their business. The silence, coupled with the sudden absence of the sounds of fighting, made a walk through any German town an eerie experience. The "sacred soils" of Germany had begun to feel the harsh hand of anger imposed by the wrath of would-be conquerors. The spectacle was not pleasant to behold.

The scene is the same familiar confusion of war and peace. Our guns were located near a turn row on the edge of a wheat field on the outskirts of Buer. The soil was thawing in the warmer weather. These soggy fields made maneuvering large guns difficult because of the mud. Our commander's strategy with this advance was to deal with the German forces in the Ruhr Pocket by encircling the German units with two deep thrusts, as on the map on p. 88.

Our advance into Buer was part of a seven-army advance directly into German defenses. The drive started with massive artillery barrages on March 28, 1945. The Ninth Army had already reached the Rhine opposite Düsseldorf and continued north to join Canadian forces. Our Ninth Army had also captured the Rhine city of Muenchen-Gladbach, the home of Nazi propaganda minister Joseph Goebbels and one of the largest Nazi cities on the western front captured up to this point.

War comes to Germany. Source: European Stars and Stripes, *March 3, 1945, 1.*

The Ruhr Pocket under siege. Source: European Stars and Stripes, *March 6, 1945, 1.*

One day we found an old man walking aimlessly through our firing zone. We caught him by the arm and led him out to safety. I asked him about his town and if he knew Goebbels. He had gone to school with him and remembered the boy with the big round eyes and big mouth. There was a castle over to my right called Schloss Rheydt, which was the castle the Nazis had told the people of the city to give to the Goebbels out of gratitude. This town put up stiff resistance before it was captured, and the castle was never damaged.

After leaving Duisberg in total ruin from our air bombardment and fighting over the past three days, it was almost gratifying and a relief to enter the Rhine city of Krefeld. The city of about 120,000 had not been attacked by our bombers, so things were pretty well intact. Most of the stores in town were open. German women wearing overcoats were riding bicycles down the streets while carrying shopping bags. Businessmen were walking around with their briefcases, although they were all old men. I noticed wide-eyed men and women standing on street corners, looking indirectly at us, seemingly surprised that they were not all being massacred. The hands of little children went up halfway in an attempt to wave before they caught themselves and followed their elders' example of looking but not acknowledging our presence. I had never witnessed a scene like this before. The city was like an

CHAPTER 5

oasis, entirely intact with business going on as usual in the midst of ruins. When our forces had attacked on this morning, all the communications were intact, and food and water were in abundance. It took only one day for our forces to take the city.

As we approached the prime city of Düsseldorf, now in rubble, the sudden appearance of SS battle groups inside the city ready to mount fierce counterattacks caused anxious moments among our commanders. The end result was nearly three weeks of difficult and costly action in terms of lives lost. Although some towns and villages surrendered at once, the defenders of Düsseldorf made a fanatical last stand. Eighteen divisions and three weeks were required to end all resistance, but the scale of our victory astounded our commanders. By April 18, three German armies had been trapped and 317,000 German prisoners, including twenty-five generals, had been taken. When the all clear was given, I took a brief walk to get a clear picture in my mind of how a city could be totally destroyed under wartime conditions.

While walking, I saw an old man on the opposite side of the street. I crossed over to meet him. He appeared to be in a numb state, as if he had been hit by a shell, and was walking aimlessly. As I got near him, I asked him if the city would ever be built up again or whether a new site would be selected. He said, in fairly good English, that it would be rebuilt. As though to prove his point, he pointed to some women already cleaning bricks on the bombed-out buildings.

I returned to my gun position after about ten minutes of walking and immediately received a fire mission. In concert with the XVI Corps, we fired all night in troop support to silence incoming artillery barrages. It was about 4:30 A.M. when I received a cease-fire. My crew were exhausted, but we were fortunate in that there were no wounded. Tired and hungry, we all went to a makeshift mess hall. I was about half finished eating when I had the urge to go back and take a good look at one of the trails of my guns, which seemed to be shifting in the soft mud as a result of the constant firing all night. If this were the case, the guns would not fire true, as the trail would shift off center. After examining the trail for fifteen minutes, I began to make my way back to the mess hall.

As I was walking along, something hit right at my feet, and the splash literally covered me from head to toe with mud. I looked around to see what had happened and discovered that a German 88-mm artillery shell had landed almost between my legs. Fortunately, it did not detonate and explode. Instead, the fuse of the shell landed in the soft ground on a flat trajectory and, as a result, did not have the force required to detonate. That soft wet soil, which moments before I had wanted to curse for throwing off my gun trail, had actually saved my life. If the shell had hit the ground at just a slight angle, it would have exploded. A section chief, who had been having breakfast, was watching from the mess hall and saw what happened. He came rushing over and gave me a piece of cloth to clean my face, as the mud had temporarily blinded me. I think I was involuntarily shaking. I was led to our medic clinic, and two hours later I was put on a jeep bound for a rest and rehabilitation camp in Belgium. The army sent soldiers who had undergone extended combat stress there for rehabilitation, usually for a week or more. This incident added to the other occasions in recent months that I had cheated death. Four hours after I left the field, I was sitting in the office of an army psychiatrist in Belgium.

The next page shows a photo taken after my first psychiatric session in the rehabilitation clinic. The date was April 24, 1945. For all practical purposes, the war was over for me. The doctor demanded that I remain in a quiet, restful environment for at least seven days. On April 25 our corps split up. Some elements fanned out in the Ruhr Pocket to eliminate resistance pockets, while the others continued on to the Elbe River. These elements did not cross the river because of the advancing resistance forces from the east. While our forces cleared up the remaining resistance in the western part of Germany, the Russians attacked Berlin in a fierce battle. Inside the city, Adolf Hitler and a few of his followers were sheltered in a bunker deep beneath the Reich chancellery. Berlin was turned to rubble as German units resisted to the very end.

When the city surrendered on May 2, three hundred thousand Russians and an unknown number of Germans lay dead among the ruins. Two days before the fall of Berlin, Hitler committed suicide. Despite the fact that he was dead, German soldiers still fought fanatically until the end. Many German units fought their way to the west to surrender to American or British units so as not to fall into the hands of the Russians.

On May 4, 1945, German forces in northern Europe surrendered unconditionally to Field Marshal Montgomery. Three days later, the remaining forces in the west surrendered to General Eisenhower's staff. On May 7, General Eisenhower announced that the mission of the Allied forces in Europe was complete. May 8, however, was designated as V-E (Victory in Europe) Day. In some remote areas, fighting continued until May 11.

Nazi Germany had been destroyed. After six long, bitter years, the war in Europe was over. Members of our army picked up copies of the *Stars and Stripes* proclaiming V-E Day as they came off the press.

CHAPTER 5

During my stay at a rehabilitation camp in Brussels, Belgium, May 1945.

The task of the ground soldier who carried the war to the enemy had been successfully completed. Supreme Commander Gen. Dwight D. Eisenhower's determined stewardship of a complex and, at intervals, contentious coalition force made the successful conclusion of a difficult campaign possible. We, as indomitable ground soldiers, transformed the possibilities of high-level decision making into victory on the ground. This, in spite of incredible harsh weather, difficult terrain, and an astute and determined foe. From my point of view, our infantry had the most difficult role to carry. General Eisenhower once wrote that it was his infantry who had demonstrated the real heroism, which is the uncomplaining acceptance of unendurable conditions. But for their part, captured German soldiers often claimed to be most impressed not by American armor or infantry but by our artillery. They frequently remarked on our accuracy, the swiftness with which we acquired targets, and especially the prodigality with which artillery ammunition was expended. The fact that the liberal use of artillery saved countless American infantrymen seemed to escape many Germans, perhaps because it cost so many German lives. Despite my ability to recount its events, my journey through this war still remains for the most part truly beyond description.

When the public announcement was made that Germany had been defeated and had unconditionally surrendered, the Belgian people poured into the streets dancing for joy. I first experienced that strange scene of the confusion of war and peace as the jeep returning me from my rest stop in Belgium entered Germany. As we drove along, I kept watching brigades of women in the hollow streets clearing rubbish from bombed-out buildings and craters half filled with water. There were more women brigades out on the streets than usual. The women had plow shafts in their hands and were walking behind the white oxen in an attempt to turn the half-frozen soil. They never looked up as we passed; they just kept slogging along. The black-and-white dairy cows that ran in terror when I last saw them a few weeks earlier kept walking among the trenches and half-frozen pastures in search of grass. As I rode along, I kept thinking how quiet and eerie it was, even with people going about their daily business.

Yes, it indeed was all quiet here on the western front. I recalled the time when I had left Germany about six nights earlier. I thought that hell itself had invaded and Satan had taken over our planet. Then the war was over and I had survived. I was saddened when I thought of the mother of the dead American soldier in the cart; had she received the news yet? The little blond boy on the hospital boat who looked perfectly normal and wanted to live so badly but just died uttering not a word of complaint. The other youngster who died while trying to lie down. The young dying tanker in the forest asking, "Where were you last night?" The face of the young German girl on top of the pile of dead. The German woman minus legs from brutal artillery fire, her face in the mud. All of these faces are etched in my memory and linger with me today after all these years.

Upon arrival back at my unit, I found my battalion preparing to leave Buer to begin security and military government duties in the vicinity of Bad Lippspringe. On May 16, 1945, my battery was relieved from attachment with Provost Marshal XVI Corps Artillery to establish local security in the vicinity of Brakel, Germany. Twenty-four prisoners of war (POWs) were evacuated to Vennebeck on May 16, bringing the total POWs evacuated to 366 and closing all POW camps in the vicinity of Brakel. Our battalion received orders to proceed by motor march to the German Ordnance Proving Ground near Hillersleben to arrive on May 31 for the purpose of calibration. All but thirty-eight rounds per tractor of 4.5 ammunition were turned in to ordnance. Battery C moved from Beverungen and established local security in the vicinity of Brakel. On May 30, the British relieved our battalion of all security and military government duties in the vicinity of Brakel. Calibration previously scheduled for May 31 was canceled by order of the commanding general. Orders were received on May 31 from the commanding general, XVI Corps Artillery, to move to Passau, Germany.

After three days in Passau, we received orders to leave and take a position in Altheim, Austria, to perform further security duty. Since all of our field artillery pieces were turned in, our mode of transport shifted back to rail on the "8 chevaux ou 40 hommes" boxcar. On June 5, we loaded our duffel bags on a waiting train and headed for Altheim, about three hundred miles north. Our required gear at this point was our green work uniforms, steel helmets, and carbine rifles. We rode all night, arriving in Altheim about 11 A.M. on June 6, 1945. D-day had been exactly one year ago. On our trip we passed through a part of Germany that was hardly touched by the war, which included the Black Forest and the area of Berchtesgaden, where Hitler's hideout was located.

There was a feeling of peace and tranquility when contrasted with the Germany we had just left. Upon arrival at the small village of Altheim, we were taken to two large farmhouses where my battery would live. A small creek ran in front of our house; on the other side was an open space of about five acres that was crowded with German prisoners. A low electrical fence bordered this area. The prisoners were in a destitute state with little food and few toilet articles. Commerce between the prisoners and the guards quickly began. We traded K rations, butter and bread, cigarettes, and chocolate bars for German pistols and various trinkets and souvenirs. They had been our bitter, faceless enemies on the battleground, but now they simply appeared human in their quest for basic necessities for survival. After discovering their desperate need for food, I found myself trading K rations for things I did not need or want, just so that they could have something to eat. For some reason, the fact that some of them had committed atrocities mattered little at the time—maybe because I already knew that they would all somehow pay for their crimes.

We stood guard all night and made regular rounds of the perimeter of the compound. About halfway down one side of the compound was a shallow drainage ditch leading under the wire fence and out of the compound. The drainage ditch was approximately two feet deep and about four feet wide. Grass was all around the ditch in an effort to prevent erosion as the water flowed through. At night I would occasionally check with guards at different points to be sure they were alert in the early morning hours. There were no lights around the compound, so security guards carried flashlights. I noticed that on some mornings, the grass in the bottom of the ditch was flat, but I assumed that it was from the rain—some nights it rained hard enough for the water to rise six to eight inches in the ditch. One night, however, while making my rounds, I happened to shine my light toward the drainage ditch and saw a flash. It was a reflection of the steel plate that German soldiers had around the heel of their combat boots. I discovered a German prisoner trying to escape. He was about fifteen feet outside the compound and the fence. He jumped up, ran toward me, and yelled, "*Nicht schiessen!*" (Don't shoot). I directed him to lie down, and another guard searched him for a weapon. He was then taken to the compound headquarters and reported as "trying to escape." I discovered that the reason the grass was flat was that prisoners had been escaping at night.

Three weeks after our arrival in Altheim, a tank company was assigned to assist us on security duty two nights a week. On one night when the tankers were on duty, a prisoner was caught about twenty feet outside the fence line. The tanker killed the attempted escapee while he was lying down without even giving him the opportunity to get up. I disagreed with the policy of the tankers. Even though it was legal to kill a prisoner attempting to escape, the war was over, and these prisoners were desperate men just trying to find food and return home. The tankers were later relieved of security duty in Austria. We remained in Altheim for another six weeks, and the security duty became routine.

On July 14, our battalion received orders to move somewhere in southern France. We cleaned up our housing and all the surrounding area, washed our clothes, and prepared for our journey across Europe. Only the people who owned the house we lived in came to say good-bye. The morning of July 16, we mounted the railcars and headed for southern France. By sunset we reached the site of Hitler's Berchtesgaden. Our train stopped to refuel, so we unloaded to stretch our legs and look around. Berchtesgaden is located on the top of a mountain and was commonly referred to as the "Eagle's Nest." There were five or six German teenage girls at the small train station. Two of them came over and explained what the Eagle's Nest was all about. They pointed out the ledge that extends out from the house—from this ledge you can look out over four countries.

By this time it was dark, and the red light on the last car of the train was all I could see. Keep in mind that when we got off the train, it was for just a few minutes, so we did not have our helmets or carbines. I was talking with the girls and heard someone call me from the train saying it was time to go. I said, "I'll be right there." Someone called a second time saying the train was leaving. There was another chief of section with me, and as we turned and looked toward the train, all we saw were red lights of the end car moving away. We immediately started running toward the train and got to within about five feet of the end car when we stumbled and fell. We both ended up on the ground as the train picked up speed and pulled away. Neither of us had our helmet or gun, and it was against the law for a soldier to be drifting around unarmed. We also had no knowledge of where the train was going.

There was a highway about a half mile west of the railroad tracks. We decided to get to the highway and attempt to catch a ride in the same direction as the railroad tracks. A truck came by about 9:30 P.M. and gave us a ride to the next city, which was Munich. We arrived in Munich about 4:00 the next morning. Our greatest fear was being arrested by the army military police for being improperly dressed. The wee hour of the morning saved us. I inquired at the station if a trainload of soldiers had been through. It had not, and the station was only a barely operating bombed-out shell. We went back to the highway to try to get a ride to the next city—Augsburg. A truck picked us up at about 4:45 and dropped us off at about 8:30 at a point near the train station. We walked over to the station and waited to see if the train would come through. At about 9:00 A.M., I saw a train in the distance. As it approached, I saw a soldier from Battery A standing beside the train door. I knew then that we had made it and caught up with our train. We had missed the train at about 9:30 the previous night, followed the highway that always remained near the railroad tracks, and found the train around 9:30 the next morning. I had never been happier to see a train.

We rode the train all day and night and arrived at Marseilles, France, the morning of July 18. In Marseilles we were assigned to single-story barracks with a common shower located in the center of the barrack. After getting settled, the first thing I wanted to do was take a shower. I stayed under the shower for about twenty minutes, and as I walked out the exit door, I met my brother Charles coming into the shower. I had not seen him since early 1942 when he was sent off to war in North Africa with the 23rd Division. I could not believe my eyes. We spent only a few minutes together because my fallout meeting was to begin in fifteen minutes. I did not see him again as a soldier.

I knew our fallout meeting was important because it was about the breakup of the 777th Field Artillery Battalion. The war in Japan was still going on, but the army had a policy that African American combat units were broken up overseas before they got back to the United States. All the ticker-tape parades down Broadway and the troops marching to receive glory from a grateful public were made up of white units. The U.S. public knew nothing about the heroism of the African American troops of the 969th Field Artillery, who helped stop the German attack in the Battle of the Bulge, where during the early phase of the battle many white troops deserted out of fear of the enemy and where the first hanging of a U.S. soldier for desertion in one hundred years took place. It was during this same engagement that the African American battalion, the 333rd Field Artillery, fought to the very end and was nearly demolished by the Germans.

Zelmo

Now a word about my cousin Zelmo. On the misty, cold morning of Saturday, December 16, 1944, some five hundred thousand German soldiers suddenly attacked American forces located in the Ardennes region of Belgium and Luxembourg. (The following discussion of the German counteroffensive relies heavily on Charles Whiting, *Ardennes, the Secret War.*) At exactly 3:30 A.M. on this cold December morning, the complete length of our front suddenly erupted in fire and flame. The weight of artillery from three German armies, ranging from 16-inch railway guns to 3-inch mortars, descended on the startled Americans of the four divisions holding the line. German infantrymen dressed in white uniforms emerged from the forest after blending with the snow, cheering as they moved forward in a half trot. Then the tanks, hundreds of them, began to rumble forward. All of a sudden the firing ceased, and there was a stunned silence as the survivors, with ashen faces and unspoken questions in their wide eyes, attempted to collect themselves. The only sound was that of the enemy's breathing and their boots as they crushed against the frozen ground with each step. Some were almost running as they moved westward. By now it was daybreak, and individual shafts of sunlight were visible on the eastern horizon. It was about 5:30. Then, all of a sudden, the entire horizon lit up as if an atomic switch had been flipped.

It was at this time that the first ghostlike figures in white camouflaged caps began their slow, ominous advance, twenty abreast with their weapons carried at high port. Elements of five U.S. divisions plus support troops fell back in confusion at the German counterattack. Two regiments of the 106th Infantry Division, cut off and surrounded atop the mountainous Schnee Eiffel, surrendered after only brief fighting, the largest battlefield surrender of U.S. troops during World War II. The African American troops of the

333rd Field Artillery Battalion faced the initial onslaught of the German counteroffensive that Saturday morning and were overrun by superior forces. However, Charlie Battery engaged the enemy, killing hundreds before most of them were cremated by enemy rockets in their gun pits.

The number killed, wounded, or captured of the 333rd was so high after it was overrun by the Germans the first day that it was decommissioned as a field artillery unit. The battalion was assigned new duties, such as guarding government installations and documents considered vital to the government and manning roadblocks in strategic places of military interest in Germany.

No one knows what happened to my cousin Zelmo, as he could not be located or identified after the rocket attack on his gun crew. No one is sure how he became a patient in a Veterans Administration mental health facility, and no one knows how and when he escaped the carnage that Saturday morning, December 16, 1944, as there were no immediate reports of the number of survivors. The only thing we know is he is in the Veterans Administration psychiatric ward today, fifty-five years later. He was never well enough to go home.

His brother, Clinton, saw him a year ago as he was standing on the corner of Dowling and Scott Streets in Houston, Texas, a primarily colored neighborhood in the Third Ward. Clinton got within five feet of Zelmo when Zelmo looked around, saw Clinton, and ran. He is an old man now, and he just kept running. His short gray hair was plastered down to his head in the style of his high school class at Smithville Colored High during the 1940s. His neck was scrawny and too small for the collar of his loose clothes. He seemed to have shrunk. The determination we had seen in his eyes of yesteryear was gone. It had evolved into sadness and hopelessness, but he still seemed alert with the quickness of a cannoneer. Clinton said he wore a Veterans Administration hospital uniform and looked very sad. He scarcely recognized him and was surprised to see him, because no one in the family knew where he was. We thought he was killed and unidentified during the German initial assault that Saturday morning. He had not been seen since he went away to the war more than fifty-five years ago. As youngsters, Zelmo, Clinton, and I would sit at the feet of Uncle Anderson, their father and my uncle, and listen to his exploits as a World War I soldier in France. None of us had any idea that a similar fate would ever befall one of us. Unfortunately, Zelmo is a mere shell today. The war imprisoned his mind but left his body whole, and he has been forced to live in this agony since then. What would have helped him come back from the brink of madness? Perhaps nothing;

but maybe Zelmo needed what we all did after our terrifying time there—the appreciation and acknowledgment from a grateful public of a job well done. The point of all of this is to make known my feelings about the army policy of deactivating African American combat units overseas and not giving them the opportunity to be thanked by a grateful American public.

Although the story of the army experience of two colored Americans setting out with the same objective but with a great divergence in outcomes makes interesting as well as informative reading for the general public, the point of its focus is too sobering and disturbing a story to be considered mere pleasure reading or entertainment. Even though the brutality of the overrunning of Zelmo's battery by superior German forces occurred more than five decades ago, the crippling, degenerative way the carnage short-circuited the permanent mental capabilities of young soldiers under stress is a heartbreaking, vivid, and powerful saga that is still pertinent today. This human story has never been told but needs to be; it is indeed a sad one. Zelmo's final life outcome is sort of a mystery. I hope to see and talk to him just once more.

On that gray, gloomy Saturday morning when the world of Charlie Battery and Zelmo fell apart, the top brass played, as described by Charles B. MacDonald in *A Time for Trumpets—the Untold Story of the Battle of the Bulge*. If at the front on Germany's snowbound western border the millions of soldiers, British, French, Canadian, and American, under their command fought and perhaps died that day, they played. After all, it was a Saturday, wasn't it?

CHAPTER 6

To the Pacific and the Philippines

I was informed at our fallout meeting that I had been reassigned to the 4416th Quartermaster Battalion. This battalion was stationed at Manila in the Philippines, and my ship was to leave that night. I packed my duffel bag and at 3:30 P.M. boarded a truck loaded with soldiers headed to the port of embarkation about thirty miles away. My seat was on the end at the tailgate of the truck bed. Just before our truck pulled off, I turned to say a final word to some members of my gun crew who had been standing in formation. We pulled off, and I never saw them again as soldiers.

At the port, the transport vessel SS *Sea Pordre* was anchored and waiting. I went aboard about 8:45 that night, three hours after my arrival. As I approached the gangplank to board the ship, I observed how tall the ship was. As we boarded, soldiers directed us to the lower decks and sleeping quarters. Our bunk beds were stacked eight high. I recall sitting on my bunk, but the excitement I had experienced on my first transport ship was gone. In fact, I felt tired and relieved that the killing had stopped on one front and was winding down on the second. We pulled offshore about midnight, and I fell asleep soon afterward. Before I knew it, a bell was sounding and it was time for breakfast. The night had passed very rapidly, and I had slept straight through. The sea was calm. I walked to the top deck my first day aboard and saw the familiar scene of the sun rising seemingly from the ocean. Later that afternoon I watched the sun set, again seemingly falling into the ocean. The big difference from my first ocean crossing is that we were all alone. Our ship was sailing on a zigzag course to avert the possibility of a submarine attack. The SS *Sea Pordre* appeared to have been traveling faster than ships in convoy. The speed of our vessel was part of its defense. The atmosphere among the soldiers on deck was more relaxed, but the different army gear everybody was wearing was a constant reminder that we were headed to a war zone.

We did not know how long we would be sailing to our undisclosed destination. Finally, we heard an announcement over loudspeakers that we were approaching the Panama Canal. This indicated to me that we were headed to the Pacific Ocean and the Pacific war zone. Going through the locks of the canal was both a historic and an engineering lesson for me. I had never imagined that a ship could float from one ocean to another with two different sea-level elevations.

Just before we cleared the Panama Canal, rumors circulated on the ship that the Japanese were about to surrender. However, our ship kept its course, headed for some unknown port in the Pacific Ocean. Two days out of the canal we were called on deck for a ceremony. The captain called our attention to the "Domain of the Golden Dragon," which extended greetings to all soldiers aboard on this day, August 17, 1945. The point of significance was that we had crossed the international dateline at latitude 32° north, and by appearing before the "Royal Domain," we were found worthy as voyagers of the Far East and were thereby conferred all its silent and honoring degrees. It is customary for soldiers to participate in this ceremony whenever they cross the international date line.

A day later on August 18, 1945, the news was announced on our ship that the Japanese had surrendered and the war was over. The Instrument of Surrender was signed on September 2, 1945. In spite of this announcement, our ship kept on course. Three days later, we arrived at the port of Manila. I was met at the port of embarkation by an officer from the 4416th Quartermaster Battalion and was later assigned to it. My stay in Manila was more of a voyage and rest period for me, as there were no specific duties assigned. I spent time trying to get to know the Filipino people. My experiences here were very different from those encountered in Europe. This was a friendly environment with no restrictions on interpersonal relations with the Filipinos.

Soon after my arrival, one difference I found was that all soldiers lived in tents rather than barracks. The mild weather made this living style possible. After I was assigned to a tent and had unpacked my bag, my German souvenirs were stolen. I discovered the hard way that you had to be careful. However, the Philippines was a friendly country, which made a big difference. I met a girl named Felicia under interesting circumstances.

In the evenings I would go walking along the beach or stroll up and down the main avenue. A lot of clubs along the avenue catered to soldiers, but they never caught my attention. I usually walked alone. This environment was really good for me, as it had all the ingredients necessary to relieve some of my stress and bring me back to the level of a normal human being. The thirty-day sea voyage had also been helpful. One day as I was walking among some homes, which were built on stilts and had thatched roofs and bamboo

CHAPTER 6

siding, I heard a noise as if someone were hitting the side of a wooden house. I stopped, looked in the direction of the noise, and saw a girl beating her long hair against the boarded part of the wall to their home. This was part of the process of drying her hair after she washed it. This hair-drying phenomenon was something I had never seen before, and I found it fascinating. I waited until she had finished and introduced myself. She was a beautiful girl, a little taller than most Filipino girls. She had a medium complexion and was study-ing to be a nurse at a local teaching hospital. I kept an ongoing relationship with Felicia and her family during my stay in the Philippines and became very fond of her. On weekends, Felicia and her younger sister organized picnics and hikes for entertainment. We often discussed the possibility of becoming romantically involved. She was willing to consider relocating in the United States.

The army had introduced a policy of discharging soldiers from the army based on a point system. Among other factors, high points were assigned for combat experience, which sent me to the top of the list quickly. My total experience in Europe and marginal points received from my travel to the Pacific theater of operations gave me enough points to be discharged almost immediately. I was happy about this because I would be home soon, but I still wanted additional time in the Philippines to develop a lasting relationship with Felicia. The happy ending was not to become reality. At this point my luck ran out.

Voyage Home and Discharge

On January 1, 1946, I received orders to report for a voyage to the port of debarkation in San Francisco. On my last evening in Manila, I went to say good-bye to Felicia at the hospital where she was training. I told her that I would see her again soon. She was saddened that my sailing orders came so quickly. I boarded a waiting army transport plane to San Francisco that same night and continued on to Fort Sam Houston, Texas, where I was dis-charged on January 6, 1946. After receiving my discharge papers, I walked out and sat for a moment on the same bench I had used when I reported to the army three and a half years earlier. It occurred to me that the time cycle was complete, beginning and ending at the same spot but covering a war that had encompassed traveling both the Atlantic and Pacific oceans. My medals—which included the American theater campaign, European theater campaign with three Bronze Stars, Asiatic Pacific campaign, Good Conduct Medal, two overseas service bars, service stripe, victory ribbon, and a certificate of merit for combat command—came off. I remember having a green stripe about two inches long on my left sleeve just below the round circular patch representing the Ninth Army. A lot of questions developed about what it represented. I would simply reply that it meant "combat command," which was technically correct. This particular identification had been instituted during the later stage of the war.

My thoughts drifted back to three years earlier when I sat here not knowing what the future had in store for me. My life had been spared on several occasions, the most recent on the last night of the war in Europe, when I was splashed with mud from head to toe from a German 88-mm shell that failed to explode. I was thankful to be home alive, safe and unharmed. Soldiers began streaming by me. I asked one about the direction to the bus station. That was where they were headed, so I followed them. My bus fare home was $3.80. I purchased my ticket and went aboard. Most of the passengers were soldiers headed home after being discharged. It was easy to separate the younger stateside recruits from the more mature, seasoned combat soldiers. The seasoned soldiers were all quiet and anxious to get home. My parents did not know that I was coming home and were surprised to see me. My brother Charles had not been discharged yet. My mother cried for joy. My sister, Volma, was away at Tillotson College in Austin, so I borrowed my dad's car one day and drove over to see her. We had a joyous sister-brother meeting. My last communication with her had been the postcard I wrote her two years earlier. We had a wonderful reunion.

Volma and her female roommate, called "Bill," had theater tickets, so I enjoyed my first movie in about four years. There is a hill in Austin called Mt. Bonnell, which is sort of a lovers' lane. Couples go there to overlook the Austin landscape at night and to be alone. Bill made it a joyous first night at home for me. It was near the close of the first semester at Tillotson College. Bill did not return for the spring semester, so I never saw her again. I also returned to college for the spring semester but in a different city and in the opposite direction. It was just after midnight when I started my drive home that night. I remember I kept thinking how fortunate I was to still be alive and how relaxed I felt in the presence of a female of my own race. In interpersonal relations, Europe and Asia had been a totally new experience for me. I drove home slowly, just reminiscing. It required two hours to make a normal forty-five-minute drive. The day had been a dream come true for me.

After my absence of three and a half years, I found my dad at his same occupation, hauling cedar logs to the mill and scrap iron to Houston. He had hired labor to replace the help Charles and I gave him. His main hand was a laborer called Midnight. In the colored community, if you were light skinned, they called you "Red"; if you were dark skinned, you were called "Blue"; and if you had really dark skin, you might be called "Midnight." My dad left Smithville at the usual hour of about 3:00 A.M. with his load of scrap iron headed to Houston. Leaving in the very early morning was a good time to drive on the highways to avoid the law. Troopers frequently stopped truckers like my dad for minor violations, such as a taillight out. They usually charged the trucker fifty or sixty dollars for the violation. The trucker expected to get about one hundred dollars for his load of iron. Sometimes when my dad got back home, he just broke even after paying for fuel and for someone to help.

On this particular trip to Houston, he left home an hour earlier in order to be at the junkyard at daybreak. This allowed for an early return home. He picked up Midnight, and they were on their way on Highway 71. About seventy miles from Smithville, he crossed the Colorado River and entered the small town of Columbus. After crossing the bridge and making a sharp left turn, you are back on Highway 71. There was a service station located to the right as you came off the bridge. It was about 4 A.M., and my dad said

My mother, very pleased to have me home again after my discharge from the army, January 1946. The house in the background is my boyhood home. This was my second day home and just before my return to college. Here I am readjusting to civilian life and wearing civilian clothes again.

he was finding it difficult to make the turn or even to stop. Before he knew it, his vision was blurred and he had collided with the service station; he had had a stroke while attempting to make the turn. Midnight was sleeping but awakened after the collision. He could not drive a car but somehow managed to get the truck, loaded with scrap iron, back home. My dad was permanently paralyzed on one side from the stroke, but he continued to work with this serious disability. A few weeks later I returned home to visit him.

Daddy was sitting on the front porch of his home when I arrived. He had been to church and still wore his Sunday clothes. We had a long, pleasant visit the rest of the afternoon. Later that night, he started to feel a bit ill and walked over to his sister's home. The time was near midnight, but his sister was still awake. He told her of his discomfort, and they were walking out of her front door to go to a nearby hospital. Daddy walked as far as the front porch and fell dead. My aunt called to tell me about my dad's sudden death. Funeral arrangements were carried out, but I never saw Daddy again. I do not look at my dead relatives.

I will always remember working with my dad when he was strong, robust, and very active. I have dreams of him after all these years, but in my dreams I never get close enough to him to see his face. After his death his various enterprises fell apart, and his assets were sold off. Recently the homestead was advertised for sale, and a down payment has been made for purchase. It seems as if the lifestyle I was brought up with has ceased to exist. Its demise started earlier when I went away to college and into the armed forces.

Heading Home, Heading North, Heading Out

I was eager to return to college at Prairie View A&M University, which I attended before entering the army. (The name changed from Prairie View A&M College to Prairie View A&M University during the three years I was in the army.) I enrolled during January 1946, the second school semester, and graduated with a bachelor of science (B.S.) degree in plant science a year later. During the registration period I looked around, and with a few exceptions, the same group that assembled on the tennis court just before our departure going into the army was registering along with me. One-fourth of the 777th Field Artillery was here. It was a happy reunion. During the semester, one of my classmates who was a former 777th Field Artillery member told me he had a hometown female friend that I should meet. I kept telling him I would like to meet her, but my heavy class load kept me engaged. During spring break, I finally met his friend, a senior home economics major named Hattie Balfour. Hattie was from Columbus, Texas, just seventy miles down the Colorado River from where I lived, meaning we had similar backgrounds. Hattie was a beautiful girl, and I felt comfortable with her right away. We were married on August 24, 1947, about ten months after graduation. We had both gone to small towns in East Texas to teach. I went to Centerville, about 125 miles from Houston; and Hattie went to Malakoff, some 210 miles from Houston. Since we graduated in January, we both started teaching immediately after graduation.

I had planned to teach at my first location for eight months and then shift to a similar teaching position near my hometown in Bastrop County. I applied for a position I knew was vacant in Bastrop County and went down for an interview during one of their board meetings just before school started for the fall semester. On the eve of their meeting, the board president asked me to wait in the adjoining room, and I would be called in at some point during the meeting. I could hear their discussion. Toward

May 19, 1947, just after my discharge from the army, while in school at Prairie View A&M University and about the time of my marriage to Hattie.

the end of their business session, the board president brought up the teaching position that was vacant and stated that there was an applicant for the position. The classes I would teach were composed essentially of veterans returning from the army who were in need of additional academic work and skills. This position also included the responsibility of maintaining the health of farm animals by vaccinating them against harmful diseases and insects, a process that required good hand skills. The board president pulled out my résumé from my prior job and proceeded to read it. My prior supervisor said, "Owens is a smart teacher in two ways. He has good academic credentials and hand skills; he works hard and is very dependable, but he also has characteristics unbecoming for a Southern Negro." One board member intervened and asked what he meant. Another board member replied, "It means you have to watch his activities in and outside the classroom." The board president pointed out that I was raised in the next town in the same county and would live there, so monitoring my activities would not be that difficult. He continued, "With proper motivation, Owens's skills would be an asset to the county program." Therefore, he recommended that the board accept my application. The board voted and approved my employment. The president then called me in and introduced me to the board. He informed me that

Hattie L. Owens, May 1948,
during our early years of marriage at
Prairie View A&M University.

I had been approved for employment and could start the beginning of the fiscal year, which was in ten days. The board then asked if I had any comments of acceptance.

I stood and thanked them for the opportunity to meet with them and for their acceptance of my application for the teaching position. I pointed out that I was a veteran and had just recently been discharged from the army. As I also had just recently married, I was leaving my prior job to be near home and my wife and family. I also wanted to work to improve the lives of a few of the veterans whom I knew. My prior job was for a short period, just eight months, but it was a good learning experience for me and a real pleasure. I made friends that would transcend time and be part of my life forever. My preference was still to come back to my home county and work; however, the monitoring constraint imposed on my employment was unacceptable. They looked around at each other and were surprised that I had overheard them deliberating the terms of my employment. I further stated, "I give one hundred percent effort in whatever I do, and my prior employer could attest to this. I must have the total confidence and trust from my employer. I was prepared to give your veterans and the county my very best. Again, I want to thank you for this opportunity." I walked out without listening to their comments.

Heading Home

While sitting and listening to their discussion of my résumé, I came to the conclusion that my life standard had to be raised, and any success that I might anticipate depended upon it. While driving home that night, among the Lost Pines, I was able to put a face on my life's objective, which was changing as new opportunities were presented. Graduate school became my focus. It occurred to me that my time in the armed services would provide me opportunities that few people dream about and seldom ever see. When I arrived home, I told my Hattie that I was hired for the teaching position but rejected it and gave her my reasons. I asked her to keep her teaching job as an income source while I returned to school.

Fall semester 1947 would start within ten days, so we had little time for preparation. I enrolled in the graduate program at my undergraduate school, Prairie View, and during the year I applied for admission to the Ph.D. program at several universities throughout the country. I applied first to Texas universities but was rejected because of my race. Even with the best of credentials, no Texas tax-supported university would accept my application for admission to its graduate program. In fact, I found out that the state was willing to pay part of my expenses to go to an out-of-state graduate program, and I accepted. Surviving in graduate school alone is difficult enough; a racist system increased my risk of not succeeding. I was accepted at most of the midwestern graduate programs I applied to and finally chose Ohio State University. As valedictorian of my high school class, I had received an invitation from Ohio State for enrollment as an undergraduate on May 13, 1940, the night I graduated from high school. I did not accept their invitation because we were too poor to pay the fees, but they still kept in touch. The fact that a big Northern university wanted me carried a special meaning and magnified my perceived worth. During the spring semester of 1948, a year after enrolling in Prairie View's gradu-ate program, I received a master of science (M.S.) degree in economics.

I did not attend summer school in 1948. In September 1948, I was employed by Prairie View as an instructor in the Department of Eco-nomics. I had my first experience teaching at college level as a graduate assistant while working on my master's degree. I found that I enjoyed the challenge of college teaching and was anxious to continue the learning process. I looked forward to enrolling in the upper-level graduate courses at Ohio State. I taught my economic classes during the 1948 fall semester and 1949 spring and summer semesters. In addition to my teaching, much of the summer of 1949 was spent in preparation to move to Columbus, Ohio, for enrollment in the fall semester.

We Head North—Graduate School

On August 15, we loaded up our car and headed for Columbus. Ohio State accepted my enrollment in their graduate program in economics based on my having completed the B.S. degree plus twelve semester hours of graduate work. An additional year of mathematics was required with one or two courses at the undergraduate level. I found myself in a transitional period, and all of these courses were of great benefit to me in my adjustment back to an academic environment.

Our drive to Columbus was enjoyable. It was my first trip with my new wife. We had been married almost a year but were teaching in small towns hundreds of miles apart, so we did not see each other that often, only short weekend visits during our first nine months of marriage. On the first day we drove about five hundred miles from Smithville to a motel in a small town near Little Rock, Arkansas. This was the only motel that accepted colored travelers, and we were lucky they had a vacant room.

The two of us had breakfast the next morning at the motel and got an early start. We enjoyed the scenery across Tennessee and the greening across Kentucky and into Ohio and finally arrived in Columbus about 7:00 that night. We easily found our living quarters, just eight blocks from the university campus. The first thing I noticed the next morning was a change in the flora, such as cherry trees loaded to capacity with cherries. The next morning we walked around the campus and then followed up on some employment opportunities for Hattie. She found a job in a bridal shop at one of the large department stores. With her employment and my assistance from the GI Bill, plus what Texas was paying for me to leave the state for graduate school, I could attend Ohio State as a full-time student carrying a load of fifteen quarter hours of course work. By being on campus a few days early, I had a chance to meet my adviser and get my schedules and books before classes started.

We leased a house about ten blocks west of campus. This was an exclusive Caucasian neighborhood where just one African American family lived. Our living here denied us the opportunity of becoming familiar with activities of an African American community in the North and its social structure. The civil rights movement was beginning to become more active, but our association with it was minimal because of academic demands.

A week after our arrival, registration and physical examinations began. The physical examination reminded me of the army in that groups of about four hundred students lined up, stripped in a large gymnasium-like building, and passed through a series of doctors who examined them from head to toe. Of the four hundred students, I was the only one who was colored. The thing I remember most from the physical examination was other students coming up to me and asking which gymnasium I used to work out. They were referring to my muscular build. The truth is I had never been in a gymnasium. My build resulted from cutting cedar logs most of my life with an ax and handsaw. This was my muscle-building regimen.

When classes started, I was anxious to test myself against white students at a major national university. I had no prior experience with white students. In fact, the only competition I had ever had against whites was as a soldier on the firing range in advanced artillery training and in sports events. We beat them in everything, but I thought the competition was unfairly in our favor. Most of my battalion had some college training, but most of the whites had only a high school education. The white college-trained soldiers had become officers, whereas for the most part, the colored were held back as noncommissioned officers.

My very first class was my most memorable. My adviser, Professor McBride, was the instructor. On the very first day, he arranged the students in the class alphabetically—I was between the students named Outhouse and Pool. I remember he posed a question before the class and I raised my hand. The answer came out and class went on. He raised a second question, and several hands went up, but mine was first. He called on me again. I went to the board but knew only half the equation he was requesting. I felt terrible about class that day. That incident taught me to be more reserved and not to jump into any discussion without full information. Ohio State operated on the quarter system, which means the pace of the classes was much faster than the semester mode to which I was accustomed. Before I knew it, we were preparing for our first examination. I thought I was ready and went into the examination with confidence. When our test papers were returned, I had made a score of 89. I did not know how my grade compared with the others, so I looked around to my left and Pool had a grade of 76. Outhouse, to my right, had a grade of 91. I made up my mind right away that a grade lower than Outhouse's was unacceptable, and I was determined to equal or better his grade. The median score for the class was about 76. During the coming weeks I worked very hard, being very careful with details and not leaving a stone unturned. I kept my hand down in class, but when I was called on, I gave well-thought-out, detailed answers. Time for the second test came around, and again I was sure of my outcome. My second test score was 92. A sneak peek and Pool had 84, but Outhouse had 94. I scored 95 points on our third and final test. Pool scored 85 and Outhouse 96. The class average was 82. Pool received a final grade of B plus, and both myself and Outhouse received an A for the quarter.

I gave the class my best shot and really tried to overtake Outhouse. I never beat him, and I am not sure he ever knew I was trying so hard to outscore him. I frankly think, from our daily conversation, he was coasting along. He worked hard but without the special effort that I put forth. In spite of our making A's in the class, I thought his superior numerical grade would upset me, but somehow it did not. I eventually learned that his undergraduate finance degree was from New York University, where their undergraduate classes had a close link to Wall Street activities. The financial significance of Wall Street was emphasized to me, for the first time, in the class; so the one-point difference was in the background between the two of us. This, I thought, would not be lasting.

At the end of each quarter, graduate students would go to the office of the dean of the Graduate School to receive their grades. I received an A minus for my first quarter. The dean congratulated me for my work, and I appreciated and enjoyed the compliment. I worked very hard for the next three years just to receive the dean's congratulations each quarter. I also received congratulations from the Veterans Administration after they reviewed my grades at the end of each quarter. After a little more than three years, I walked across the graduation stage with M.S. and Ph.D. degrees in economics with a finance minor.

My GI financing ran out one quarter before my graduation, but I had performed so well that the government assisted me financially through graduation. After walking across the stage and receiving my degrees, I felt both elated and a little disappointed. I had always thought that after receiving a Ph.D., I would be knowledgeable about most everything—with an understanding of literature, a reading knowledge of foreign languages, and the ability to be a great researcher. The disappointment was that I discovered there was so much more to learn. I started thinking, while onstage, that I had come a long way and the forces of circumstance had come together to make an almost impossible dream come true. My service to my country provided the financial assistance necessary for me to make this leap, coupled with a university that opened its arms and gave me a fair and equal chance to achieve my goals while universities in my own state deprived me of the same opportunities because of the color of my skin. Finally, the comments of the county board president that night served as a catalyst for me to achieve something greater, forcing me to raise my sails and flow into deeper water for my life's work. *Indeed, it is not the gale but the set of the sails that determines the direction you take.* For all of this, and my beautiful wife's encouragement and financial support, I am privileged and truly grateful.

The time spent at Ohio State was both educationally positive and enjoyable. My professors of whom I have complete memory include Dr. Wirth (finance); Dr. Sherman (prices); Dr. Faulkner (economic policy); and Dr. McBride (marketing), adviser and major professor, who died before I completed my doctoral program. It was in his class that I embarrassed myself on my first day in class by being overaggressive in responding to questions he had raised. I recovered from that error and moved on. The three African American graduate students enrolled in the same area of concentration as myself were Allen Felder, from Virginia Union University in Virginia; George Dowdy, from Tuskegee Institute in Alabama; and Johnny Smith, a former member of the Tuskegee Airmen during World War II. I did not come in contact with any of the African American undergraduates because they were so few in number at the time, although the enrollment began to increase toward the end of my tenure at Ohio State because of concerted efforts by the university to recruit minority students. Robert Dorsey was an African American undergraduate student who graduated the semester before I entered the graduate program. He was an all-American defensive end on the Ohio State football team and graduated with a civil engineering degree and a 4.0 grade-point average. We had played football together at Prairie View in 1942 before the war. James Tucker, another friend who played football at Prairie View in 1942, went on to the University of Pennsylvania, received his Ph.D., and became a regional director for the Philadelphia District of the Federal Reserve System.

The four professors mentioned earlier were very helpful in steering me through my course work during my three and a half years at Ohio State. On one occasion, I was a participant in presenting a seminar with two other graduate students, Merrill Evans and Elmer Bonner, both of whom were white. At the end of the presentation a question session began and *75 percent* of the questions were directed toward me and my portion of the presentation. My professor explained what he thought were the reasons why I received the highest concentration of questions. He said, first, I had a quality presentation with good information they wanted to know more about; and second, they could not understand everything I said because of my Texas accent. This presentation occurred early in my academic program at Ohio State, but I did not try to change my accent. I just spoke more slowly.

My African American friends all graduated on time. Allen Felder went to India as part of the U.S. Aid program; George Dowdy returned to Tuskegee as head of their Economic Department; I am not sure of Johnny Smith's final outcome. Elmer Bonner, one of the white participants in our first seminar, became dean of the Graduate School at Ohio State. I do not know Merrill Evans's final outcome, but I am sure it was positive because he was a bright student.

Twenty years after my graduation, my son Emiel Jr. expressed an interest in enrolling in Ohio State to work toward a Ph.D. in mathematics. Elmer Bonner assisted with securing the necessary admission applications and in granting him a scholarship. Emiel Jr.'s son or daughter will likely in time matriculate at Ohio State, all because of the university's propensity of expressing kindness toward strangers.

During my last year at Ohio State, our first daughter, Shelia, was born in Columbus. After graduation we took a two-day vacation to Niagara Falls. It was late evening when we arrived at the falls. Our young daughter really enjoyed this sight and kept pointing to the water flowing over the falls, which left a mist and a rainbow of colors. Our tour guide told us a fascinating legend about an occurrence on the falls. A man and his son were crossing above the falls with a boat pulling a barge loaded with hardware. They were riding on the loaded barge when it pulled loose from the boat and started drifting toward the falls. They could not get off the barge that night as it approached the falls. Just a few hundred feet before reaching the falls, the barge lodged on a rock. All night the two thought the barge would dislodge at any moment and tumble over the falls. The next morning when the man and his son were rescued, the father's hair had turned from black to white and the son had lost his mind. If you visit the falls today, more than sixty years after this occurrence, you will see the same barge lodged on the rock.

On the third day, we began our journey back to Prairie View where I secured a position as assistant professor of economics. Our second daughter and two sons were born while we were at Prairie View.

During my fourth year at Prairie View, I was recruited to go to Liberia, West Africa, with a team of specialists to develop an academic institution in a small tribal village called Kakata. This town is about fifty miles west of Monrovia, the capital of Liberia. There was an existing institution in Kakata, but our duty was to develop it into a full-fledged technical institute with a wide range of subject matter and skill offerings.

It was only yesterday, as time goes, that America reached out into the wide avenues of world production. This section presents a brief history of the little-known, small republic of Liberia, a nation in miniature established by freed American slaves at the western extremity of Africa more than two hundred years ago. From its inception Liberia has been regarded as a moral protectorate of the United States, as throughout its troubled history it has received our support and encouragement.

I left Prairie View on June 10, 1957; went to Washington, D.C., for a one-day briefing; and then on to New York. On the evening of June 11, I left New York on a fourteen-hour flight to the West African city of Dakar, where we refueled and then flew to Roberts Field in Liberia. I was met at the airport by a delegation and driven to Booker Washington Institute near Kakata, where housing had already been arranged for the families of the technicians. Six months after my arrival, I was joined by my wife, Hattie, and our three preteenage children, Shelia, Angelia, and Emiel Jr. My first impression of Liberia as I drove the seventy-five miles from the airport to our future home was that it was a beautiful country, with greenery everywhere; but judging from the appearance of the people we passed on the road, it was an impoverished country. The natives swept the dirt floors of their huts with brooms made of local palm tree branches.

My second observation, as we drove along the graveled main road, was that women were the beasts of burden. They transported heavy loads of goods such as food items, neatly bundled, on their heads. I noticed that the average African woman walked erect with exposed breasts. The women were not at all self-conscious until they noticed that we Americans were staring at them.

Upon arrival at Booker Washington Institute, I was taken directly to our specially prepared living quarters. They were modern, two-bedroom apartments well equipped with standard electrical appliances. The exterior walls were white stucco, which means they stood out distinctly from the surrounding houses for native workers and their families. We had our own generator for electricity. Since only the American technicians lived here, some "redline" tension developed quickly between the technicians and our African counterparts. "Redline" means to discriminate against in housing or insurance by withholding funds for home loans and insurance from neighborhoods considered poor economic risks. White lenders in the United States tended to redline poor black neighborhoods, and this practice was transported to Liberia by some American blacks.

I took a walk from our housing community to the village town of Kakata on my first evening in Liberia. I wanted to find out something about native life, such as how they live and their social structure. All I had observed up to this point was native men and women walking on the roads. The female was always a few paces behind the male, and she was the one to transport items on her head. It was late evening, and the men were sitting on stools in front of a row of thatched houses. I could hear them speaking to each other in their native dialect as I approached. It was a funny thing. Here everybody is black, but that is the only thing we have in common. We neither look alike nor speak alike, and our background is totally different. I continued to walk to the next group of native homes, observing construction styles and any peculiarities.

One common thread stood out in the construction of all the homes. Attached to the main circular structure of each home was a lean-to. This lean-to or room contained a bed, a wooden stool, and a small table. Everything was constructed of unfinished native wood. I later discovered this was a guest room for walking travelers. Liberians contend that walking travelers always have food because of the abundance of fruit along the way, and they also always have somewhere to stay because of these guest rooms. The travelers may or may not contact the owner of the guest room when they come in at night or during the day. The room is simply home for a night. I was really struck by this concept. When I built my home in Texas, an extra room somewhat separate from the regular family activity was included for friends or strangers so that they would feel free to stop at any time.

I continued to walk through the compound. A very large drum, about three feet in diameter and ten feet long, was in the center of the houses. Drums play an important role in the life of an African man. Messages are sent on drums of this size. Travelers may send messages to the next village, and emergency messages are transmitted by drums. All of the drums are hollowed out of tree trunks or tree branches.

Approaching the next set of houses, I heard music. Glancing inside, I saw a man beating cymbals to a fast rhythm while people sang and clapped. In front of what looked like a pulpit, a small band was playing with guitars made of wood and steel strips. Others were standing in a half circle, picking guitars in a trancelike stance as if they were around a throne. They began to chant with the same dominant rhythm of a song I heard when I first entered the compound. It was a love song about marriage called "Nana Kru":

I can see your ma and your pa
They tell me they want me for their son-in-law
Brought four cows, six goats, and fifteen sheep
And now they tell me you're mine to keep
Oh, Oh Nana, Nana Kru
Nana, Nana Kru
Jump into my canoe, dear
I paid my dowry for you
Nana, you're my wife in ladies way
Government make one new law out of day
Say two dollars and fifty cents they want me to pay
And go to government church in Christian way
Oh, Oh Nana, Nana Kru
Nana, Nana Kru
Jump into my canoe, dear
I paid my dowry for you.

As I was approaching the last house at the end of the compound, I was told one of my counterparts lived here and was ill. No one could enter his home to treat him. One young man standing nearby said that the man was suffering from a severe case of diarrhea and was now having dehydration symptoms. He had brought three chickens into his home, which supposedly would cure his diarrhea. I left the village and went back to my apartment where I had medication. I sent him the amount needed, which cleared up the problem almost immediately. After this occasion, he always thought I was some sort of miracle man. This small act set the stage for a good future working relationship. He later became his country's representative to the United Nations.

A week later, as I was passing through Kakata, I saw four or five people with belts and switches striking a boy as he hastened down a path in the village. I found out later this was the compound's way of administering law and order. The boy had stolen some fruit from a tree and was caught leaving the village with it. This form of punishment was cruel but effective.

I discovered I could observe evolution taking place right before my eyes in Liberia. Tropical climates such as Liberia's have two seasons, dry and rainy. During the six-month rainy season, the natives fish in streams for a certain type of fish. During the dry season, when the streams run short of water, the same fish will burrow down into the sand on the banks of the streams. Therefore, the natives dig for fish during the dry season.

One of my assistants went digging one day and filled a five-gallon container with this special fish. He took them home and left them in the bucket on his back porch where it was cool. He planned on cleaning them later. He sat down in his living room, which was about thirty-five feet from the porch, to work on some reports. He told me he kept hearing a noise but was so engrossed in his work that he did not stop to investigate. Later, as he turned to pick up a sheet of paper, he saw one of his fish on the floor. It had leapt from the bucket and propelled itself all the way across the wood floor. In terms of the evolutionary process, in time this water/land fish may well become land borne; it will adapt to living on land and leave the water.

On my third day in Liberia, I organized my classes. I had prepared for my first class meeting and wanted to make a good first impression. It turned out to be a mild disaster. The class had already assembled when I arrived. I thought they were as anxious to see and hear the new professor as the professor was to meet them. I passed out my syllabus, introduced myself, and began the class discussion by talking about why we were here for this course. One of the students introduced the concept of how humans have strived to survive and maintain a family structure. I then made the statement that the difference between a civilized and native man is that the civilized man domesticated animals, which meant his family's survival was not directly dependent on a kill at every hunt. If a native man did not kill at every hunt, his family would have some hungry days and would suffer the health consequences. Nearly all hands went up after this statement. It turned out the problem was one of semantics. I had used the terms *civilized* and *native*. These words had a very different meaning among Liberians.

When African slaves were brought to the United States, some were offered, by organizations such as the Quakers, the chance to return to Africa after gaining their freedom. Many slaves accepted the offer of money and ships and returned. They landed on a small island just off the mainland of Liberia. After going ashore, they named their capital "Monrovia" after James Monroe, the U.S. president who allowed them to return to Africa. The Africans that had been taken as slaves to the United States and returned to Liberia were called "civilized," and those who never left Liberia were called "natives." The returning slaves took charge of the country by organizing the government and setting the laws and policies, both monetary and fiscal. It was not a democratic society in that the civilized sector remained in power perpetually. In time, this became a source of friction because the native majority sector thought they were being exploited by a small minority sector. Thus, one sector turned against the other in tribal, economic, and social wars.

I was corrected in my interpretation, and we had a good discussion. That early incident was good for me because it forced me to take the time to learn about the customs of the students along with their areas of sensitivity. I must say that my two years of teaching experience in Liberia was perhaps the period of the most growth that I had ever experienced. You cannot isolate teaching experiences from those encountered in daily life. These include health, communication, living hazards, and a social life with your students and the inhabitants in general.

My feelings were also changing. For the first time in my life I began to look at the world through the eyes of a white man. By this I mean I was part of the majority; everybody around me had a black face, from the government officials to the lonely people I saw walking on the street. All decisions were made by blacks. We had met the president and were invited to his mansion on several occasions, where we discussed economic and financial issues. We were part of the discussion, and our input eventually became part of the monetary and fiscal policies. The few white faces I saw in such settings were in the minority, a direct reversal of the historical position of black Americans in the United States.

The time passed quickly, and my classes grew larger and more interesting. Some suggestions made about monetary and fiscal policy were initiated, and the Liberian economy grew rapidly. Our fourth child was conceived in Liberia but born in Texas, as my wife returned home before delivery. My two-year tour of duty sped by. The development of Booker Washington Institute, our target institution, was on schedule. It is a great training institution now. We had a banquet celebrating our success the night before my departure back to the States. The minister of education and the president of Liberia, who had recruited Prairie View A&M University to develop the institution, were our main speakers. I was presented a special award for services rendered. It had been a real privilege for me and a truly great learning experience. I left by plane the next morning to return to my teaching position at Prairie View.

Back to Prairie View

Upon my return home, I needed a few days to get reacclimated. I slept a lot, and it felt good to be home. I must admit the ten years after my discharge from the army were perhaps some of my most productive. I established myself as a faculty member at Prairie View, attended graduate school for almost four years, worked overseas, and began my long-term permanent employment. I had succeeded in elevating the plane upon which to start building my life's work and was happy about it. I found a bright group of students to work with at Prairie View, so I set my teaching research program in motion. I was able to experiment with many of the theories I had been taught in graduate school. The university employed public transportation to take my students on long field trips in connection with classes in marketing and finance, such as a bus trip to the Texas Rio Grande Valley to study the integration of productive pricing and marketing.

The university furnished a small duplex apartment for on-campus housing, but as my family continued to expand, we purchased land and built a home that was suitable for our family needs. In fact, we established the tone for a quality level of private ownership of homes in the community.

To the University of Minnesota

During the first year after my return from Liberia, I wrote a paper about the monetary and fiscal policy strategies of Liberia and submitted it for presentation at a meeting of the North American Economic and Finance Association (of which I was a member) held in Sydney, Australia. En route to Sydney, I took a side trip to Tahiti. I was joined by twenty-nine other delegates, who were mostly from the Midwest, specifically the University of Minnesota. It was a delightful group, which made the trip very restful and enjoyable. In general discussions during breaks at the conference, many of the Minnesota professors invited me to come to their university and spend some time as a visiting professor. I said, "I'll think about it."

Upon returning home and after discussing the opportunity with my wife, I told the chairman of the department at the University of Minnesota that I would accept their offer to spend two years as a visiting professor for the fall semester beginning August 1970. I would go without my family because three of my children were in school. My oldest daughter, Shelia, was going to attend the University of California on a special scholarship, called the Chancellor's Award, granted by the governor, Ronald Reagan. Hattie was employed as a middle school teacher at Prairie View.

Upon arriving in Minneapolis, I was immediately aware that it was much cooler than Texas. I found my living quarters and unpacked. The next morning I met the department chairman and received my teaching assignment for the semester. I started teaching on August 17, 1970.

My first class was set for 10 A.M., so I had a little extra time for preparation. At about 9:45 that morning I left my office for class, which was to be held in the same building but in a room in the far north wing. To get to the classroom, I had to go down a long hallway and past the office of the department chairman. As I neared his office, I was walking and looking down at a note I had just added to my lecture. When I became even with the door, I heard the chairman call my name and say, "Emiel, I need to see you for just a minute." I cautioned him that it was class time, so it would be better if I talked with him after class. He then said quietly, "I just wanted to let you know that your class is all white and they have never had an African American professor. In fact, most of them have never been around a black person." Before he could complete his sentence, I cut him off and told him I did not want to hear it and cared even less. I told him I could take care of myself, even though I appreciated his concerns.

Those comments stunned me. I thought they were unnecessary coming from the chairman. I hesitated momentarily before entering the classroom as a lot of things quickly flashed through my mind. I was thinking that Vern, the chairman, really thought he needed to say what he did. He thought it was the right thing to do because, in my estimation, Vern was one of the most honest individuals that I had ever known.

I had not looked at my roll sheet before entering the class, but I assumed that I had a typical junior-level class of between forty and fifty students. Instead, as I walked in, I found the lecture room was a large auditorium with about four hundred white students, not a single face of color in the room. There was a stage for me to stand on, and therefore I was talking down to the students. I took a few seconds to let them get accustomed to seeing an African American professor and then introduced myself. I will have to admit that what Vern said quickly flowed through my mind, but just as quickly it left.

I began the lecture by discussing the objective of the course, the role economics plays in our daily lives, what the students should expect from the course, and my expectations of them. The room was very quiet by this time. Strangely quiet. I really believe it was so quiet I could hear the sound of their pens writing. What had happened was that I was shocked when I first walked in, which forced me to draw from all my teaching resources and fall into a rhythm of teaching that almost mesmerized the students. I broke the silence by raising a few questions about points presented in my lecture.

A teacher always knows the sixty- or ninety-minute class period is up when students begin to shuffle papers and prepare to shift to another class. This never happened. I kept them right down to the last minute and actually had to tell them it was time to go. As they left class, some came by and said they enjoyed the lecture, and I thanked them. There was no class following mine in the auditorium, so I waited a few moments before leaving to pull my thoughts together. This morning had been a new experience for me. No matter how long one has been teaching, each new group of students is a new experience. My first African class was a new experience, and this large all-white class was a new experience. I discovered that good teaching techniques, coming from a broad base of experience and hard work, transcend groups, whether large, small, black, white, male, or female. One or two of the students in the class worked in the chairman's office. I learned that they had made very favorable comments in the office about my lecture, such as that I had raised the art of university lecturing to a higher dimension and stimulated their interest in learning about economics. I was pleased to know I had been able to communicate at our first meeting. My challenge now was to keep up the pace and to continue to broaden the learning environment.

My next task was to complete my ongoing research. I had a research paper that had been accepted for presentation at the forthcoming European Agricultural Economic Association Conference, which was to be held in the Soviet Union on November 27, 1971. I also had been selected to chair a session at the conference. Hattie accompanied me on this trip to the Soviet Union. Our delegation was briefed by an expert on Russia about the dos and don'ts once you enter the country. Our flight to the Soviet Union started in Minneapolis; stopped in New York where an additional 175 delegates came aboard; and then continued on to Zurich, Switzerland.

As we deplaned in Zurich, we saw the Russian jetliner parked on the runway. We were directed to a terminal building to wait until we boarded the Russian plane that would transport us to Moscow. Our total delegation to the conference was in excess of 200 from all over the United States. It was interesting to observe how the Cold War affected our sense of reasoning. We all kept looking at the plane with suspicion and talked among ourselves about how we doubted the capabilities of the Russian pilots and plane to transport us safely the few hundred miles to Moscow. The discussion became so intense and vocal that no one was allowed to point out that this Russian airline transported more passengers for longer distances than any other airline in the world and should be capable of transporting our delegation a few hundred air miles. We had about a two-hour wait during which time we purchased soft drinks and enjoyed the mountain scenery and cool fresh air surrounding the airport.

By that time our flight was ready to depart, and we began lining up to board. Most of our apprehensions had been quelled, and we were ready to continue our journey. The sound of laughter and friendliness was back among our delegates.

I remember boarding the plane and noticing that the interior was very practical but simple. All the seats could be folded into various combinations of seating and sleeping arrangements for short and long trips. I also remember the Russian-speaking attendants coming by my seat offering assistance. The attendants were all white with blond hair, but their facial features were different from those of the whites I was accustomed to seeing primarily in Texas. They seemed so foreign, as if from another cultural universe, and all they were doing was going from seat to seat offering their assistance to make us comfortable.

After a two-hour flight, we landed in Moscow. We boarded a bus and were transported to our hotel, where we received our room assignments. I found again the rooms to be adequate but quite simple. The floors were made of a low-grade marble and were clean yet unpolished. There was adequate hot and cold water for showering, but we had to purchase bottled water for drinking and for brushing our teeth. There was no TV, but classical music was piped into each room. Our meals, taken in the hotel, were good and included a wide range of foods. The meals tasted like the food prepared by my grandmother in iron pots on wood stoves but with interesting different seasonings and styles of preparation.

My session in our economic conference was scheduled for 10:00 the next morning, so I spent the evening in preparation before deciding to take a short walk along the canal just to the east of the hotel. I went to bed early to get a good night's rest and catch up with my jet lag. All the conference sessions were to be held in different rooms and lecture areas in the hotel. It was a matter of walking up a few flights of stairs to get to the individual sessions, as very few elevators were available in this massive hotel. My session began on time. Mine was the last of four papers to be presented; the other presenters were from Greece, Germany, and Russia.

The Russian presenter caught my special attention, although all presenters had interesting, thought-provoking papers. The Russian presenter was a woman from Siberia. Her paper was on migration, but what caught my attention was the mathematics she used in defining a social science problem, which I had not observed before. When she stepped before the group to make her presentation, I noticed she was poorly dressed and used no makeup. From her general appearance and before her presentation began,

I had the impression that the quality of her work would suffer the same fate as her appearance. My impression changed once her presentation began, and I became fascinated with what she was saying. In putting the migration model together, she used an algorithmic strategy she called "pattern recognition." I did not recognize this algorithm being utilized in finance or economic literature. After the question-and-answer period was completed, I asked her to send me a copy of her paper and gave her my home and office addresses. She informed me that three months earlier she had presented the same paper at a meeting in Poland. It was written in English, and she would be happy to send me a copy.

At the conclusion of the conference, Hattie and I decided to take a trip to Leningrad and visit the world-famous Hermitage Museum. We took an overnight train from Moscow to Leningrad. The train was a sleeper car in which four people occupy one booth containing two double bunk beds. We occupied one of the beds, and a couple from Finland occupied the second. Once again, the train system was adequate but very plain and simple. We enjoyed our overnight train ride and the company of complete strangers. We took a bus from the train station to the hotel where we had made reservations. We spent our first day viewing some of the world's greatest paintings at the Hermitage. I especially enjoyed the work of the French artist Gauguin. I had read of his painting *Yesterday, Today and Tomorrow* and now was able to see it firsthand.

We had tickets to a concert hall called the Gypsy Palace on the first night and heard Gypsies sing in concert. I found the music and the songs to be very different from any music I had heard previously. It was very entertaining but sad. It was pointed out, later on, that most of the Gypsy music was played on guitars, in minor chords, sad chords for sad songs. In many ways, this music reminded me of the old cotton-field blues, where a worker was saddened because of a loss, usually of a woman, and expressed the depth of his hurt in song.

The guitars the Gypsies used were of special interest to me in that they were strung with seven rather than six strings. After the concert, I decided to go backstage and ask one of the guitarists whether the seventh string was a bass or treble string. The first guitarist I encountered did not speak English. As I tried to communicate with him, I mixed sign language with an occasional English word. I spoke and made sleeping signs with my hands on the side of my face to him, saying, "We are here in Leningrad for just a few days and are sleeping at the Hotel Leningrad." He thought I said, "While we are here in Leningrad, we have no place to sleep," so he beckoned to his wife and caught our hands, indicating that we should come stay with them while in Leningrad. I wanted to go for the experience, to learn something about how they live and maybe get a lesson on how to play a seven-string guitar. However, Hattie disagreed, thinking it would be too risky. I thanked the guitarist the best I could and again told him we had a place to sleep.

We left the Palace and walked to the street to catch a cab. After we had waited about three minutes, two people in a car stopped and offered us a ride to our hotel. We accepted and had an opportunity to engage in conversation, as they spoke some English. I think they were studying English at the time and used this opportunity to practice. They were a young, delightful couple, and it was a good experience for all of us. At the hotel, we thanked them and offered them compensation, but they refused, so we simply wished them a good night. It had been a very good day.

On our second day in Leningrad, we toured the city and attended a circus and a concert in a rural community. The singing group was composed of approximately sixty male and female workers from all the surrounding farms. They sang primarily Russian folk songs. I particularly enjoyed this group because the talent of the working-class people was being used. We spent another day and night in Leningrad after which we returned to Moscow, joined our delegation, and left the next morning for the United States. When our plane cleared the runway in Moscow and became airborne, our delegation cheered. From the tone circulating, I got the impression that it was a political cheer, so I did not join in. I had a wonderful tour, one I thoroughly enjoyed. The people had been very gracious to us. Upon our return to the United States, Hattie continued her trip back to Texas and returned to Prairie View.

About three months later, I received a package that contained five articles from the Soviet Union. I noticed right away the return address of my section presenter. An hour after I received the papers, the FBI was in my office wanting to know what the package from the Soviet Union was all about. They wanted to know if they could come by my apartment during the evening for an interview. I granted them the privilege. During the evening interview, they desperately tried to link the academic discussions to economic outcomes. I was finally able to convince them that I had no interest in the economy of the Soviet Union, but I could use the academic contribution in further describing social science issues in the United States and around the world. After about three hours we broke off our discussion. They gave me a copy of the tape recording, and we said good night.

CHAPTER 7

Meeting a New Visiting Professor

The chairman of my department introduced me to another visiting professor, Adolph Weber, from a university in Kiel, Germany. I had seen him several times at some of our international economic conferences, but we had never been formally introduced. About a week later I visited his home and met his wife, Geshiel, and his two preteen daughters, Reglendia and Ruthild.

We both had just been introduced to the computer; thus, we spent long evenings in the computer room learning programming. I was often invited to their home for special holidays and for dinner, as I was alone without my family. I found the Webers to be simply delightful people.

One evening, while visiting their home, a discussion of World War II came up. I think it was in the context that I had been to Germany, so someone asked when and under what circumstances. I mentioned that as a soldier during World War II, most of my time was spent in western Germany in the Ruhr valley. I also told them that after the war in Europe was over, I was engaged in city administration and security duty, which included guarding German prisoners. Adolph said that most of his army time was spent on the eastern front in Russia, where he was wounded and ended up a prisoner of war in a camp in Austria. As it turned out, he was a prisoner in the camp in Altheim, Austria, where my unit was in charge of guarding the German prisoners. This reinforced the notion that this is truly a small world.

Our two-year visiting professorship ended at the same time, and the Webers came to Texas with me to spend some vacation time with us in Prairie View. My daughter Angelia took Ruthild and Reglendia on a tour of the campus, which included a trip to the goat center, part of the experimental station. It is the only center in the United States with a goat-breeding program, and the offspring are shipped all over the world, primarily to Africa, to be used as breeding stock. The Webers were particularly interested in this program, as it supported Adolph's work in Kenya as director of the Department of Agriculture. Later we had dinner on the patio, which overlooked a large cornfield. I had mentioned to Adolph that on some still nights I used to sit on the patio and listen to the corn grow. Dinner was served after sunset, and they had the opportunity to enjoy a phenomenon that had afforded me such pleasure.

The next day we decided to take a ride to visit my mother in Smithville. I took a secondary road through a German American community, giving them the opportunity to see what a typical German American small farm was like in this country. My mother was so pleased that they were visiting her home. My mother's style of cooking and seasoning was different from theirs, having more of a soul-food flavor, and they thoroughly enjoyed it. After about two hours of socializing, we returned home, driving through fields of bluebonnets and Indian paintbrushes. That evening the girls listened to my stereo system while Hattie and Geshiel enjoyed chatting in the kitchen. Adolph spent late hours with me on my patio. We had so many things to talk about.

On their third and final day in Texas, we left for Galveston where the water of the Gulf was warm, much different from the cold water of the Baltic Sea to which the Webers were accustomed. We had an enjoyable swim, picked up a few souvenirs, and returned to Houston for dinner. We tried to make our last night memorable and arrived back at Prairie View well after midnight.

My daughter Shelia was a student at the time at the University of California, San Diego. So when the Webers left Texas, they flew to California to spend a few days with Shelia before returning to Minnesota and then back to Germany. In our home at Prairie View, Ruthild, the younger daughter, saw a medical model of a plastic skeleton head and shoulders of a man that we had purchased for Shelia before she finished high school. Ruthild told me, in later years, that the head frightened her when she was a youngster, but it had made an impact on her choice for a life career. On her desk today, she has the same type of head and shoulder skeleton. Ruthild finished the high school equivalent in Germany and went on to medical school in Heidelberg, where she received her M.D. She is a neurosurgeon and took special training at Yale University. Reglendia finished high school and went to universities in the Rhineland where she received her Ph.D. in chemistry.

For ten years my family and the Weber family exchanged biannual visits. Our visits to Kiel were usually tied to my attendance at professional meetings in Europe, England, or Africa. My relationship with the Weber family is of special interest to me. The bond of compassion and camaraderie that has formed between the Owens and Weber families overshadowed our differences in ethnic and cultural backgrounds. It confirms our belief that all people can live together peacefully and productively when they have a will to do so. We were supposedly bitter enemies on a field of battle, with the objective and training to kill. Wars take place, and many young lives are lost; but many more survive and go on with their lives as if this awful tragedy had never happened. What I discovered after getting to know this German family was that in spite of coming from different parts of the world, with totally different backgrounds, our life objectives were about the same: earning a decent living with enough capital accumulation to afford our children the education corresponding to their academic capabilities. The Webers spent a great deal of their money and capital in developing countries such as Kenya, East Africa, trying to raise the health and living standards among the children there, as we did in Liberia, West Africa. Adolph Weber was at the University of Minnesota as a "visiting professor," the same as I was. I believe if their two daughters had lived with us or my four kids with them, their academic outcome would have been the same. What I am saying is that people everywhere seek high levels of achievement and advancement that transcend the hatred, the violence, and the evils of war.

Reglendia, the Webers' older daughter, was married on June 11, 1994, and sent us an invitation. She wrote this personal note on the back: "Dear Owens-family, Wouldn't it be a treat, if the two of you would celebrate this wedding together with us? You're very, very welcome! Love, Reglendia." Hattie, Shelia, and I attended the wedding in Bucha, Germany. The Owens family has not missed communicating with the Weber family by telephone on Christmas morning for at least twenty years.

A visit to the chapel in Bucha, Germany. From left to right: Emil Owens Sr., Adolph Weber, Geshiel Weber, and Emiel Owens Jr.

The University of Houston

My two years as visiting professor at the University of Minnesota proved to be very productive and rewarding. From a research and teaching point of view, the department was a little more provincial; however, the system was well structured, which meant newcomers to the department could adapt easily to their style of teaching and conducting research. This was essential because the University of Minnesota usually maintained a high percentage of visiting faculty from all parts of the world, and simple adjustment methods allowed them to move quickly into the department's research and teaching activities. During my second year at Minnesota, I was recruited by representatives from the University of Houston to come to the university and fill a position as associate professor in the Department of Finance. I was going to Houston at the end of the summer semester and agreed to stop by for an interview. I accepted the position and remained at the University of Houston for twenty-two years.

The three areas of concentration at the University of Houston included teaching, research, and service to the university. These same three criteria were used to determine the annual success of the program of a teacher, that is, promotion and salary increases. The effectiveness of a teacher, as evaluated by the students, became an important part of each faculty member's evaluation. Various student organizations had regular annual selections of their favorite professor.

The success of a professor's research output also was measured by published articles in recognized journals and the presentation of results at national meetings. The topic of service covered a wide range of activities, including serving on department and college committees as well as being invited to visit a country such as the Soviet Union to participate in specific development activities.

In my case, I was invited to participate with a group of social scientists to discuss the concept of credit unions to groups of rural Russian households. The main point that needed addressing among Soviet citizens was their disposable income and saving rate and the importance of developing a well-defined capital market. In this communist society during the Cold War era, there was a shortage of desired private goods, such as clothing. These goods were available but sold on a black market at high prices. The per-family income was low, but saving as a percentage of disposable income was high. As a result of this high saving rate, a small percentage of the household savings could have been deposited in financial institutions. Instead, the savings

CHAPTER 7

were hoarded and kept in various places in the home and out of circulation. The reason for this was that the public goods market was a cash market, meaning that households who wanted to participate in the private market needed to keep cash on hand. We introduced the credit union concept, where small savers could have a safe place to save and earn interest on savings and could purchase private goods at a discount from retail prices. We have not been able to evaluate the effectiveness of participation because of a lack of a follow-up opportunity.

While at the University of Houston I also was able to reach out into the community and use my economic research skills in an attempt to improve the health conditions of farm workers. I joined my brother Clarence, who had a study approved by the National Science Foundation and the Environmental Protection Agency to determine the effect of pesticides on the health of migrant workers. We traveled and lived with two migrant work crews for a year, taking blood samples and testing for the presence of organophosphate pesticides. Federal regulatory changes were made as a result of this study. We also published scientific journal articles and a book, *Peacocks of the Fields—Life of Migrant Farm Workers*. This research project was part of the diversity of research conducted through the Center for Health Management, College of Business Administration, the University of Houston.

CHAPTER 8

Summing Up

This book is about my life before and after my service in the U.S. Army. My objective has been to make a record of some of the footprints I have made over my lifetime. They were made in the context of various time periods: from my being born into the false prosperity of the 1920s and brought up in the grim reality of the Depression of the 1930s; through my active participation in the war years; and finally, through my mature adult life, including marriage, family, education, and work. I am now entering the waning years of my life—my steps are slower, my hearing less sharp, my vision blurred, and at times my memory reservoir faulty. Common ailments that my body eagerly shook off at an early age are now lingering on as a permanent component of my body's landscape. The cycle is nearing completion as I am almost back to where I started.

It is prudent, from the point of view for posterity, that I pause here and make this record of some of the various life events that impacted my behavior, and the direction I took, outside the Christian homes I was reared in, including my marriage, my army experience, educational opportunities, and work experiences. My marriage to Hattie Balfour was the crowning event of my life. She brought to it the adhesive needed to keep my floundering and illusive life objectives in focus and is the catalyst that gave me the strength to persevere at times when the odds seemed insurmountable. From the residuals of these encouragements, I learned to meet triumph and disaster and treat both of these impostors just the same.

My service with the armed forces of the U.S. Army was the second most important event that impacted my life's course. In the outlay of events with linkage to army service and being engaged in a war on foreign soils, I was fortunate enough to have survived this carnage. Today, I look back on this event as simply a part of life's passing parade, from which I learned so much. Regardless of the purpose, my having crossed two oceans and the English Channel on two occasions broadened my horizon of understanding of the world around me and presented me with an expanded vista through which to view the world and its people. I saw, firsthand, people speaking different languages, of different phenotypes and likely genotypes, but all with the same hopes, fears, aspirations, and desires to live and to work to make a living wage to support a family.

That early-morning encounter with the German family having breakfast in the house we commandeered left me with an enduring feeling, because after their fears of survival were allayed, they sat and finished breakfast. I noticed that before resuming eating, each said a prayer and they offered to share with me their egg, wheat bread, jelly, and coffee. I refused the offer but thanked them. My mind drifted back to my grandmother's kitchen table at home. Strangely, the meal, style of serving, time for reverence, and sharing were the same as at home. You may ask, how I could even think like this of my enemy? My only answer is we tend to believe at once in evil things and only believe in good upon reflection. Is this not sad?

I cannot even imagine how my educational endeavors would have turned out without the financial support I received from the Veterans Administration. Adding to my financial difficulties was my state's racist policy of not allowing African Americans to enroll in upper-level programs offered at white graduate schools within the state. Going to an upper-level graduate program out of Texas incurred a greater cost to me because of the high out-of-state expenses charged. This denial also added additional cost in my attempt to

My home at 4135 Gairloch Lane, Houston, Texas.

Dr. Emiel W. Owens in 2004 at age eighty-two.

achieve a level of education that would afford me proper employment for an adequate living standard. I have a deep and loyal feeling today toward the universities that accepted me in both their undergraduate and graduate programs, as did Prairie View A&M University. They accepted me in the raw and taught me so much. I am grateful to Ohio State University for accepting me in their graduate Ph.D. program. They showed an interest in me the night I gave my valedictory address at graduation, May 24, 1940, by inviting me to join their undergraduate program. I was unable to accept their offer for financial reasons, but they still kept in touch. They encouraged me along the way and gave me an equal opportunity to learn and achieve, according to my capabilities, the highest academic reward. For this I am eternally grateful. I follow with a passion their football team and get chills when their band strikes up "Carmen Ohio."

There is still the need for all African American children to set high goals and standards for themselves and to follow the rule, "If at first you don't succeed, try, try again." It is not failure but setting low expectations that is the crime.

When my writing is caught up, I spend my time restoring my 1950 Mercedes Benz 220-S convertible. There is an annual drive between Indiana and California that classic cars make. No car younger than a 1964 model is eligible to enter the drive. The drive crosses the most beautiful parts of this country—nature at its very best. My 1950 Mercedes Benz 220-S is right on target. It will be fun.

Because of what life has offered me, I am optimistic in believing that I have contributed in making this world a better place. We do not have the opportunity to choose our own parts in life. The fact is that we have nothing to do with selecting those parts. Our simple duty is confined to playing them well. The span of life was lent for lofty duties, not for selfishness, not to while away for aimless dreams, but to improve ourselves and serve humankind.

Bibliography

Balkoski, Joseph. *Beyond the Beachhead: The 29th Infantry Division in Normandy.* Mechanics-
    burg, Penn.: Stackpole Books, 1989.

Ballard, Ted. *Rhineland, 1944–1945.* Washington, D.C.: U.S. Army Center of Military
    History, 1995.

Bedessem, Edward N. *Central Europe.* Washington, D.C.: U.S. Army Center of Military
    History, 1992.

Department of the Army, The Adjutant General's Office, Historical Record Section,
    Departmental Records Branch, A.G.O., Washington, D.C., July–December 1944.

Dzwonchyk, M., and John Ray Skater. *A Brief History of the U.S. Army in World War II.*
    Washington, D.C.: U.S. Army Center of Military History, 1992.

Francis, Charles. *The Tuskegee Airmen.* Boston: Bruce Humphries, 1968.

Fugate, Bryan I., and Lev Dvoretsky. *Thunder on the Dnepr, Zhukov-Stalin and the Defeat of
    Hitler's Blitzkrieg.* Novato, Calif.: Presidio, 1997.

Goldstein, Richard. *America at D-Day, a Book of Remembrance.* New York: Dell, 1994.

History—777 Field Artillery Battalion. College Park, Md.: National Archives Trust Funds,
    1996.

Lewis, Jon E. *Eye-Witness D-Day.* New York: Carroll & Graf, 1994.

MacDonald, Charles B. *Company Commander.* New York: William Morrow, 1982.

———. *The Last Offensive, the Official U.S. Army in World War II Series.* Washington, D.C.:
    U.S. Government Printing Office, 1973.

———. *A Time for Trumpets—the Untold Story of the Battle of the Bulge.* New York: William
    Morrow, 1985.

Marshall, S. L. A., with John G. Westover and A. Joseph Webber. *Bastogne—the First
    Eight Days.* Washington, D.C.: U.S. Army Center of Military History, 1988.

Miller, Edward G. Preface in *A Dark and Bloody Ground: The Hürtgen Forest and the Roer
    River Dams, 1944–1945.* College Station: Texas A&M University Press, 1995.

Nelson, Theodore A. *D-Day 1944.* Lawrence: University Press of Kansas, 1971.

Neuwiller, Charlene, archivist. *European Stars and Stripes.* Washington, D.C.: Editorial
    Library, Reference Department, 1945.

Phillips, Robert F. *To Save Bastogne.* New York: Stein & Day, 1979.

Stanford, Theodore. "Artillerymen Stuck to Guns, Made Jerry Keep Distance." *Pitts-
    burgh Courier,* April 2, 1945, B6.

———. "Our Boys Fought in All Major Battles." *Pittsburgh Courier,* April 2, 1945, 7.

———. "777th Artillery Joins Montgomery's Drive." *Pittsburgh Courier,* April 15,
1945, 10.

Stone, M. P., Wayne M. Dzwonchyk, and John Ray Skates. *A Brief History of the U.S. Army in World War II*. Washington, D.C.: U.S. Army Center of Military History, 1992.

Whitaker, Denis W., and Shelagh Whitaker. *Rhineland—the Battle to End the War*. New York: St. Martin's Press, 1989.

Whiting, Charles. *Ardennes, the Secret War*. New York: Stein & Day, 1984.

———. *The Last Assault—the Battle of the Bulge Reassessed*. New York: Serpedon, 1994.

———. *Siegfried—the Nazi's Last Stand*. New York: Stein & Day, 1982.

Young, James C. *Liberia Rediscovered*. New York: Doubleday Doran, 1934.

Index

battalions. *See* field artillery

Battery A, 777th Field Artillery Battalion, 26, *61,* 77, 95

Battery B, 777th Field Artillery Battalion: chief of firing battery, 67–68; E. O.'s leadership in, 26, 30, 32, 45, 53–55, 67–68; and Rhine campaign, 3, 79–81; training of, 26, 30, 32. *See also* European Theater

Battery C, 777th Field Artillery Battalion, 26, 92–93, 97

Battle of the Bulge, 96

Belgium, 51–55, 90, *91,* 92, 96

Berchtesgaden, Germany, 93, 94

Berlin, Germany, 78, 90

Beverungen, Germany, 92

"Bill's" warm welcome home, 102

biracial child, Smithville, Tex., 6, 11, 12

bivouac training, Fort Sill, 26–31, *27, 29,* 48

blackouts in England, 40–41

blindfolded assembly practice of howitzers, 26–27

blond boy in hospital ship, 45, 92

Bonaparte, Napoleon, 81

Bonner, Elmer, 112, 113

Booker Washington Institute, Liberia, 113–18, 121

Boston, Mass., Camp Myles Standish, 36–37

Brakel, Germany, 92–93

Bricquebosq, France, 41–42, 47, 48

bridges: Rhine River, *80,* 80–81; in Roer River campaign, 72–73, *73*

Britain, Great, 39–41, 44–45

British military units, 74

Brussels, Belgium, 90, *91,* 92

Bucha, Germany, *127*

Buer, Germany, 87, 92

"Bunnie Town," Smithville, TX, **9,** 10

Burgess, George (grandfather), 31

calibration of artillery, end of war, 92–93

California, University of, San Diego, 119, 126

Camp Beale, Cal., 31–36, 53–54

Camp Myles Standish, Mass., 36–37

casualties and death: Ardennes campaign, 96–97; blond boy in hospital ship, 45, 92; burials, 62; cotton picker, 16–17, 25; D-day invasion, 42, 44, 93; E. O.'s response to, 76, 82–83; German ME pilot after ejecting, 69; hospital ship crossing English Channel, 45; Hurtgen Forest battle, 56–66, *67;* Rhine campaign, 81–83, 92; Richterich battle, 59; Roer River campaign, 65; soldier pallbearer efficiency, 63; tanker rescued by E. O., 63–65, 92; troop ship sunk by German sub, 39

Catherwickerham, Germany, 81

Caucasians. *See* whites

Charlemagne, Holy Roman Emperor, 63

Charles, Ezzard, 29

"Charlie" Battery C, 777th Field Artillery Battalion, 26, 92–93, 97

chief of firing battery, Battery B, 67–68

chief of section, Battery B, 26, 30, 32, 45, 53–55, 67

childhood of E. O.: divorce of parents, 7, 10, 19; reflections on, 8, 130; rural sharecropping life, 5–6; town life, 6–13; youth, 13–20, *20,* 108

Christmas, 1944, 66–67, 68–69, 70, 72

churches in Smithville, Tex., 10

circadian rhythms, human, 55–56

civilians, German. *See* German civilians

"civilized" as Liberian term, 117–19

father of E. O.: Army leave visit, 30–31; death of, 104; divorce of, 7, 10, 19; and E. O.'s return from war, 102–4; log cutting, 7, 20; railroad work, 6–7, 9, 11, 13, 31; sharecropping, 5–6; trucking and hauling work, 13–17, 102–3
Faulkner (Ohio State professor), 112
Felder, Allen, 112, 113
Felicia the Filipina, 101
FFA (Future Farmers of America), *21*
field artillery: assignment to, 24; calibration of, post-war, 92–93; digging in for firing, 76–77, *77*; Eisenhower on infantry, 91; German guns, 66–67, 76, 89–90, 102; 969th Field Artillery Battalion, 96; organizational structure of batteries, 26; 775th Field Artillery Battalion, 32–33; 776th Field Artillery Battalion, 32–33; 31st Field Artillery Battalion, 24, 26–31; 333rd Field Artillery Battalion, 96; tractor prime movers, 28, 49; training, 26–33, *27, 29*, 36, 53–54; 202nd Field Artillery Group, 63; weaponry types, 26–28, *27, 29*, 32, 47, 49, *49, 78. See also* 777th Field Artillery Battalion
5th Panzer Division, German, 60–61
Filipino people, 100–101
firing battery. *See* Battery B, 777th Field Artillery Battalion
1st Panzer Division, German, 60–61
fish, Liberian, 116–17
fitness at Ohio State University, 109–10
Focke-Wulf 190 (German aircraft), 68
football, 21, 112
Fort Sam Houston, San Antonio, Tex., 23, *24*, 24–26, 101
Fort Sill, Lawton, Okla., 26–31, *27, 29*, 48

4.5-inch guns, 28, *29*, 32, 47, 49, *78*
4.7-inch guns, 28
4416th Quartermaster Battalion, 99–102
France: Bricquebosq, 41–42, 47, 48; countryside and agriculture, 49, 50; D-day invasion, 41–42, 44, 46, 93; Hirsen, 51; Le Mans, 50; Marseilles, 94–95; Paris, 50–51; Saint Lô, 47
Future Farmers of America (FFA), *21*

Galveston, Tex., 126
Gauguin, Paul, 123
Geilenkirchen, Germany, 63
gender inequality, 114–15. *See also* racial issues
German-American farmers in Texas, 86, 125
German civilians: breakfast with, Dinslaken, 83–86, 131; deaths in Rhine battle, 81–83, 92; Rhine River crossing warnings to, 76; surrender and V-E Day, 90–91
German military: Ardennes offensive, 96–97; field artillery, 66–67, 76, 89–90, 102; Hurtgen Forest battles, 56–66, *67*; Luftwaffe, 68–72, 80; Panzer Divisions, 60–61; Rhine River battles, 3, 68, 74, **75,** 76–83, *77, 80*; Roer River battles, 58, 65–74, *73*, **75**; Ruhr Pocket battles, 58–90, **88**; Russian Army and Eastern Front, 78, 90; submarines "wolf-packs," 38–39; surrender and V-E Day, 90–91
Germany: Bucha, *127*; destruction in, 56, 65, 86–89, *87*; Kiel, 125, 126; Mehrum, 3, 74; Siegfried Line, 28, *29*, 32, 47, 49, 56, 74, *78. See also* European Theater; POWs, German
GI Bill, U.S., 105, 108, 111–12, 131–32

vessels. *See* transport ships and crossings

Veterans Administration (VA): GI Bill, 111–12, 131–32; Zelmo Owens in hospital, 97

V-E (Victory in Europe) Day, 90–91

walking traveler guest room, Liberia, 115

Washington Street, Smithville, Tex., 6, 8–9, **9,** 10

weather conditions: Hurtgen Forest campaign, 51, 58, 60, 65–66; and Liberian fish, 116–17

Weber, Adolph, 125–27, *127*

Weber, Geshiel, 125, 126, *127*

Weber, Reglendia, 125, 126, 127

Weber, Ruthild, 125, 126

Weier, Germany, 73

Welburn, Mit, 6, 11, 12

Western Front, Germany. *See* European Theater

West Texas cotton pick, 15, 17

West Wall (Siegfried Line), Germany, 28, *29*, 32, 47, 49, 56, 74, *78*

whites: and E. O.'s performance at Ohio State, 110–11; in 775th and 776th Field Battalions, 32–33; University of Minnesota students, 120–21. *See also* racial issues

Whiting, Charles, 96

Witmer, L.G., 31

"wolf-packs," German, 38–39

women's rights, 114–15

Woods, Sgt., 33

World War II: GI Bill, 105, 108, 111–12, 131–32; Pacific Theater, 22, 30, 95–96, 99–101; Pearl Harbor attack, 22; surrenders during, 90–91, 96–97, 100. *See also* Army, U.S.; European Theater

Worth, Richard, 77

Wright, James, 60

Yasco, 1st Lt., 30

Yesterday, Today and Tomorrow (Gauguin), 123

youth of E. O., 13–20, *20*, 108. *See also* childhood of E. O.

ISBN-13: 978-1-58544-537-0
ISBN-10: 1-58544-537-1